FINDING FUNCTION
in a
DYSFUNCTIONAL ORGANIZATION

Dr. R. N. Givhan

AuthorHouse™
1663 Liberty Drive
Bloomington, IN 47403
www.authorhouse.com
Phone: 1-800-839-8640

© *2010, 2014 Dr. R. N. Givhan. All rights reserved.*

No part of this book may be reproduced, stored in a retrieval system, or transmitted by any means without the written permission of the author.

Published by AuthorHouse 05/27/2014

ISBN: 978-1-4969-1586-3 (sc)
ISBN: 978-1-4969-1585-6 (e)

Library of Congress Control Number: 2014909677

Any people depicted in stock imagery provided by Thinkstock are models, and such images are being used for illustrative purposes only. Certain stock imagery © Thinkstock.

This book is printed on acid-free paper.

Because of the dynamic nature of the Internet, any web addresses or links contained in this book may have changed since publication and may no longer be valid. The views expressed in this work are solely those of the author and do not necessarily reflect the views of the publisher, and the publisher hereby disclaims any responsibility for them.

CONTENTS

Introduction vii

Chapter 1 How we got here? 1
I. Theorist 3
    a) Theorist Analysis 3
        1) Behavior 3
        2) Organization Structures 6
        3) Organization Processes 17
    2) Organizational Concepts 28
    3) Development of Organization 29
II. Learning in the Corporate Environment 31
Summary 33

Chapter 2 Organizations of Today 34
I. Literary Discussion 34
    a) Organization Analysis 34
        1) Definition of organization 34
        2) Levels/Hierarchies of organization 35
        3) Analysis of Organization 37
    b) Organization Behaviors 38
        1) Individual 39
        2) Group and Team 40
    c) Organization Development 42
        1) Learning 42
        2) Goal and Productivity 47
    d) Interactive and involved Leadership 48
    e) Next Generation of Organizations 52
II. Summary 53

Chapter 3 Developing a Workable Model 54
I. Organizational Needs 57
II. Change Drivers 58
    1)   Change Models 59
    2)   Constraints to Implementations 62
    3)   Application and Strategies 64
III. Summary 69
Reference 71

INTRODUCTION

The Industrial Age was a time of manufacturing development and organizational development. The Industrial Age was a large contributor to organizational foundations. During this time, manufacturing structures developed into power systems of people. This foundation allowed people to construct systems and hierarchies distributing control and over site. In the new Information Age, organizations became even more organic. The Information Age moved the organizations beyond building walls. The Information Age created organizations globally. With the broad reach of technology people and organization's desires and needs changed drastically. This has also imposed a new level of education and training on organizations. Knowledge and know –how with technical interfaces are central to organizations growth and development. Psychological understanding of individuals affects organizations now. All of these factors represent an evolutionary need in organizations and contribute to the success and failure of that organization. In many situations, most are unaware of virtual impacts to organizations. The differences of control from the Industrial Age to the Information Age cause many to fear. These concepts influence organizations in so many facets most researchers have not completed.

The layering of people provided jobs and security for many in the Industrial Age. In some regards, those systems have continued to evolve, yet in some areas those systems stall and die. Based on various areas of research theories that dictate a life cycle of an organization exist and can be revolutionary. The basis for such research focuses on the Industrial Age to the Information Age. The move to understanding that organizations are living beings and need analysis is clear. The communication of organizational surveys applies this logic. In the twenty plus years of organizations,

Dr. R. N. Givhan

listening to the employee demonstrates a supposedly growing organization. In chapter 1 of this, book an analysis of organizational theories from Etzioni, Gibson *et.l*, Hall, and Morgan. I will focus on three aspects. The organization's structure, organization's processes and organization deliverables are areas that each of the theorist discuss and develop. The comparison of these areas shows downstream movement to assisting new organizations to be successful. There is a careful regard for all types of organizations from family units to corporate systems. The corporate area is important to this writing such that implementation of the application focuses on corporate environments.

CHAPTER 1

How we got here?

Corporate organizational development (OD) in recent years has become a multi-million dollar industry. Many corporations are seeking to understand how to get efficiencies and productivity from their organizations. In recent years, the measurement of productivity is important to various nations based on an alignment to profit. In this alignment, the need for innovative environments, diverse structure of employees, and the technology changed the layout of most organizations. Having organizations that are flexible and agile enough to respond to driving forces of market analyst becomes essential in developing strong business plans. Organizational change and learning organizations are the stomping grounds for such organizations. Organization agility while embracing new technology and expansion of workforce all over the global feed this multi-million dollar industry.

The theorists provide comprehensive detail about structures of organizations, the processes within the organization and the deliverables of these organizations. The relationships of these areas provide researchers with plan implementation strategies. As it is clear that, the structure of the organization would dictate the implementation of processes, which create specific deliverables. Each theorist documents their views on organizations in functioning arenas. The perspectives communicated tell of organization evolution and paths forward. The changing landscape of industry require theorist such as Hall etc. to understand various organizational needs. There are foundational aspects to organization that each writes about and details. In most cases, these areas are individual entities there is little focus on their relationships. In addition, there is little discussion on the affects of technology in reference to organizations. Although, these theorists provide a good foundation of organizations, the discussion of organizational requirements, resources and standard implementation gave me valuable information on the formulation of organizations. The Information Age impacts discussion by Hall also establishes the need to review individual psychology within organizations. Their contributions fundamentally state defined concepts of organization life cycles.

This discussion focuses on specific implementation of strategies affecting the three major areas of organizations. The three prong approach of organization structures, organization processes and organizational deliverables. The strategies assist in recognizing problems and issues that produce dysfunctional organizations. The strategies assist in improving the organizations once dysfunctions are determined.

The three major objectives of this section are analyze the organizational theories of Etzioni, Gibson *et.l*, Hall and Morgan in terms of their underlying principles about organizations: to compare and contrast the philosophies of Etzioni, Gibson *et.l*, Hall and Morgan from their perspectives of organizational concepts: and to discuss the strengths and limitations on present applications of organizational development strategies. The theorists of this document produced writings demonstrating how organizations function and develop. The evolution of organizations continues today based on needs from industry. The theorist used within this document reviewed various types of organizations. Each developed a definition of organizations and the environment of implementation of specific organization structures. The process of implementation identified by theorist has become standard procedure for many industries. Templates provided by these theorists give insight to control needs of the organization. The theorist recognizes and discusses psychology philosophies of organization implementation and development.

I will start my communication by first introducing the theorist named in this document and then describing their theories. These theorist works focused on are Amitai Etzioni, Richard Hall, James Gibson *et.l* and Gareth Morgan. Each developed differing approaches to the growing needs of organizations. I will then expand on the objectives listed above.

I. Theorist

1) Theorist Analysis

a) Behavior

In recent years, behavior analyses in organizations are areas of concern for development of the organization. Hall and Gibson *et.l* both continue the organizational development by including key factors to the research. Emphasizes placed on behavior and lifecycles broaden the organizational impact and concept. This process of understanding individual needs and involvement is a strength to building healthy and strong organizations. Gibson *et.l* segregates himself by offering in-depth details for cognitive behavior analysis and development in individuals. The process Gibson *et.l* introduces limited behavioral model implementation. Gibson *et.l* describes techniques such as Myers-Bridges and etc. These are tools used to identify behavior patterns. Hall does not move to implementing techniques, yet he does make a distinction in behavior of management. This is within his concept of the organization lifecycle. The behaviors are contributors to the death of the organization. Hall focuses on this process of change within the organization. Hall excludes details of individual needs within the organization, yet recognizes individual reward recommendations.

Hall and Gibson *et.l* specifically acknowledge that employee behavior is a factor to the success of the organization. Gibson et.l identifies specific behavior of employees and the impact of the actions on teams and groups. Gibson et.l uses behavior models to demonstrate individual behavior influences and corrections. Hall uses philosophies of defensive routines that influence the failures of an organization. Morgan described behaviors in metaphor analogies, yet he never placed individual control over the behavior. Morgan acknowledges that employee behavior is important in learning organizations and power conflict organizations. Various metaphors used by Morgan require an understanding of the behaviors of employees. Etzioni references individual behavior based on the organization. Etzioni describes the focus of human behavior to be the concern of the Human Relations organization.

Gibson's *et.l* approach is an academic format. Three other individuals in the development of the "Organizations Behavior, Structure, and Process" join Gibson they are John Ivancevich, James Donnelly, Jr., and Robert Konopaske. In this document, I will refer to Gibson *et.l* when discussing philosophies from his body of knowledge.

Gibson's *et.l* focus highlighted the behavior of organizations. The behavior of the organization details the concepts of human interaction. The methods described by Gibson *et.l* develop connections to human psychology and the role it plays in an organization. Gibson *et.l* describes behaviors in levels. These levels are individual, team, and group. Individuals are the components of the both teams and groups.

In describing individuals, Gibson *et.l* breaks down the psychological variables that contribute to individuals' processing of information. The psychological sub-sections are perception, attribution, attitudes, and emotional intelligence. Within each, he discusses the process of analyzing individuals for group and team activities. He demonstrates the importance of evaluations and understanding of individuals by the organization. The individual must also understand the structure and functioning of the organization. Gibson *et.l* relates common factors of human motivation also. The relationship of the individual behaviors and motivation of that individual are important to the successful running of the organization. He uses Maslow's hierarchy of needs to build the relationship of individual behavior, motivation and the functioning of the organization. As well, he discusses many theorists in relationship to human behaviors; Alderfer's three level hierarchy, Herzberg's two-factor theory, and McClelland theory of learning needs. The development in human behavior allows the theorists in process the needs for control of the organization. It is clear that individuals within the organization are the systems within the system in organizations. In developing a focus on such components of the system during time of issues or problems solutions with individuals are solvable. In these sections of the book, a number of other items are highlighted in human interactions and processing. Gibson *et.l* suggests employee surveys, as well as, many other formulas in getting knowledge about the individual with the organization. Gibson *et.l* describes for the reader methods for motivating an organization. He reveals mapping techniques for awarding employees and managers. There are also discussions on negative behavior that may affect the performance of an organization. He provides a procedure to assist in modification of behaviors. Gibson *et.l* looks in detail at stress in the work environment and the affects those may have on an individual's work performance. In understanding the organization, Gibson *et.l* moves to the lowest common denominator, the individual.

Gibson *et.l* then reviews the impact of the individual with a group or team. The psychological processing of the individual seems to change based on the power structure of the team or group. He reviews the standard process for the development of teams using the five-stage model. He also defines the formal groups and informal groups, which are the sub-tier applications of the organization. The behaviors within these group and teams may be a morphed representation of the individual. The behaviors bases for the team or group members evolve from the team and group needs. A definition for groupthink as an attribute of the team describes the processing method of the team. Other dynamics that affect a team's performance, Gibson *et.l* discusses for clarification on factors that may contribute to the failure and success of the team or group. There are additional high-level interfaces that influence the functioning of the team, such as power and politics, and organizational leadership. The focus Gibson *et.l* gives to the individual demonstrates his philosophies that people are core of the organization. The attention given to behaviors, individual needs and psychology amplifies these concepts for additional researchers to understand. Gibson *et.l* believes by providing people with their internal desires and needs you will have a successful person, which flows into the output of a successful organization. In the process of understanding those needs, the focus on motivating people and groups essentially becomes the corporation's successful business plans.

With Gibson's *et.l* emphasizes individual behavior, which is a different approach from other theorist. Gibson *et.l* communicates his belief that the life and death of an organization lie in the hand and hearts of the individuals within the organization. The actions and behaviors of the individual contribute to the success and failure of the group and team, which feed into the overall organization. By understanding human psychological contributions, Gibson *et.l* is able to describe successful organizations and diagnosis issues of failing organizations. In every aspect of Gibson's *et.l* review human behavior, response and reactions are evaluated. Gibson et.l discusses analysis of management behaviors contribute organizational development and sustainment. The approach to organizational structures lay in job design and employees. Gibson's suggestion to understand the job task allows management to optimize skilled workers and establish control in completing the program or project. With a review of management comprehending the relationships, behaviors alteration with the job design and employee organization success is achievable.

Etzioni stated human relations organizations focus on emotional unscheduled organizational behavior. These have a tendency to be more social and information organizations. This organization brought to light that the worker has needs and desires. Concepts like worker satisfaction and productivity developed from these types of organizations. Etzioni references Elton Mayo in discovering four major concepts associated to worker in the emotional arenas. In the process of human relations, Mayo determined worker's needs and relationships to management on an individual or group base. The four concepts are as follows:

1. The physical build of a worker is not indicative of the amount of work they can accomplish;
2. Rewards not related to money also play a part in motivating workers;
3. A highly specialized task is not the most efficient job based on the division of labor;
4. Workers within social groups respond to management norms and rewards better than individual workers do.

As well, the roles of leadership, communication and participation emphasized the need for human relations. The roles of group dynamics became a component of human relations. This impact changed some views of structuralists. In most situations, the role of the Human Relations organization conflicts with that of Scientific Management based on the organizational goals. During this time behaviors of the individual was new to the development of organizations. Morgan does not review discuss individual behavior in the same context.

2) Organization Structures

Gibson *et.l*, Hall, and Etzioni define organizations using fundamental theorist Weber, Mintzberg, and etc. Each referred to the development of organizations and used the same concepts in job design and job categories. The bureaucratic structures and controls measures identified demonstrate organization creation, which follow standard processes. Similarities in these processes solidify the theoretical contributions. All three of these theorist approach organizational structure in the same formats. The most significant addition was Etzioni's secondary level organizational structure with the additional R, T, and L-structures. The focus of these levels emphasizes openness in charismatic structure.

Gibson's *et.l* philosophies for organizational structure development and design focus on the structure of the industry and environment. Growing trends in corporate environments are structures designed with the concepts of quality of work life and work/family balance designs. The major themes of these structures are telecommuting, flextime and job sharing. The applications of these reflect on the job requirements and job deliverables. The actual hierarchies of the organization are the outer layers of developing an organization structure. The incorporation of the concepts aligns to the desires and needs of employees. In developing these systems within the organization, Gibson *et.l* suggests completing job analyses. This would create an objective understanding of the job itself and the job requirements. The organizational structure creation is the dividing of overall task into small units for successful completion. The relationship between individual behaviors can affect the layout of the organization. The bases is monitoring and maintaining control over the organization. Management desires to influences every area of the organization dictate management layers and employees job assignments. In applying, a specific structure jobs specialties and industry influence management decisions. Gibson *et.l* provides information on the concepts of departmentalization. Gibson *et.l* comments on the differences of functional, geographical, product and customer departmentalization. Each meeting the needs of the management focuses. There are occasions when there is a matrix organization. In this insistence, a combination of departments provides a specific span of control. Gibson *et.l* identifies areas to consider in developing the organization layout and the span of control required for employee effectiveness and productivity. Aligned with the span of control the assignment of responsibility and authority reflects the needs of the organization. The power hierarchy within the structure identifies communication paths, decision paths and job specialties. Gibson *et.l* even introduces organization models. Models such as Organic use a more flexible structure where the employee moves as the product needs or company needs change. This type of organization can seem in chaos for outsiders, yet with detailed processes and procedures of implementation, they function on results bases. These models are affective based on the industry implementation. This model structure focuses on a high level of satisfaction for the employee. This system utilizes the human potential. He then references organizational processes such as integration and the development of virtual organizations. Virtual organizations have become common methods for companies with employees separate geographically.

Morgan uses the defined structures to develop systems of analysis for organizations. Morgan identifies the contributions of Weber and etc., yet his focus examines the strengths and weakness of the organizations. Morgan develops systems of implementation for the success of the organization. He discusses the lower level process used to improve employee environments and relationships. In reviewing the employee needs Morgan uses concepts of Maslow hierarchies of needs to improve environmental reactions from the employees. Morgan does not disputed the bureaucratic implementation rather he questions the format and organization emphasizes.

Etzioni approaches organizations in a different format. He first acknowledges that there are many types of organization. Each type has different needs and may require different communication methods, as well as, other processes. He defines organizations as social units purposefully constructed to meet a specific goal. He focuses on the need to group humans in a rational way, such that the appropriate production of products takes place. He describes the variety of labels organizations use to categorize themselves. Formal organizations are organizations, as well as, bureaucracy. Sometimes Institutes reference themselves as organizations. Etzioni moves away from defining detail methods to creating organizations and comments that organizations are patterns of social groups and controlled by the different methods of power. Etzioni documents that there are initially two types of organizations. These are ones formed from the Classical Theory of Administration and Human Relations. Each of which provided a method for structural approaches to developing organizations

The Classical Theory of Administration commonly known as Scientific Management, where, the environment focuses on highly skilled workers and motivational drivers are economic wealth based on production. Etzioni references the work of Frederick W. Taylor as the creation of combining motivation and organization. During examination, the benefits received by developing systems of motivation became an integral part of creating a structural layout of a good organization. The process increasing the motivation to do work aligned with two major foundations. The first being that pay bases should evolve from work performance not seniority. Secondly, hourly paying is better than monthly for disbursement of funds. He even suggested the pay based on product completion is better. All of these findings focus on industry organizations. The actual layout of the organization focuses on division of labor. The division of task down to the smallest components aligns the desired labor needs. The worker specialized in the completion of that task can develop efficiencies. This structure has a relationship of control. By breaking the task down emphasizes on control becomes simpler due to the break down. In the process of assembling the product, the control moves to a higher level in the organization each time the product moves to completion. This develops what; Etzioni calls a pyramid of control, where the control leads to the top layer, the top executive. Based on the complexity of the product the organization takes on another line method of control. This centralizes the authority of the organization. In formulating this organization Etzioni states, "Most Classical writers, however, agreed that work in the organization should be specialized according to 1 or more of 4 basic principles" (1964). These principles align to the product need and the clientele need. Principles, 1 and 2 states for the product the task purpose should be specialized and a particular process should complete the task itself. Principle 3 states that the division of labor may focus on how your clientele structure/organization functions. Principle 4 states that task performed in the same regional area should have divisions. Etzioni remarks,"The tendency is often for the lower layers to be organized according to area and /or clientele principles and the higher ones by purpose and/or process. (1964)" Having a mix in the organizational structure may provide more efficiency. There is a requirement for control a mechanism for control is job division. By dividing the task and job, the organization provides control at all of those levels. These levels also create sections that conflict resolution can take place. The creation of a Program specific structure may meet the need to maintain goal achievement. The foremost importance is using the above stated principles in creation of the division of labor for the Program specific structure. On many occasions the more decisions an organization has to make the less centralized the authority is. Within the organization, the requirement to quickly make decisions and maintain goal alignment factor into determining whether there is a need to centralize or decentralize authority. In further analysis, Etzioni describes Scienific Management structures as bureaucracies, a term he gleamed from Max Weber. This was due to Mr. Weber's concern for the distribution of power. He further discusses how to control workers within the organization to maintain effectiveness and efficiency. His philosophy on getting workers to except rules as law with and without justification moved bureaucratic structures to Legitimation. Legitimation is the relationship between having power to control and the ability to justify. Please note that justification may not have any relationship to historical data, it is based non-relational elements. Bureaucracy structures are organizations that set norms and then enforce them. All rules and regulations must obey if the organization is to operate effectively. This structure places workers in positions to reward obedient behavior and punish those that do not. This format the organization establishes order by manipulating the workers. This process keeps the individual alienated. The entire process for legitimation builds or destroys the level of commitment the worker has to the organization. The structure provides employees with process norms. Etzioni states that Weber referred to power as the ability to induce acceptance of orders; legitimation is the acceptance of the exercise of that inducement because it aligns to the worker's value system. He also described authority as the combination of the two terms; power that deemed legitimate. Based on Etzioni's statements, Weber suggested that for organizations to be effective and efficient bureaucratic authority is a requirement. Systems with charismatic leadership are short lived, as stated by Etzioni. The belief is that the division of labor lacks stability or specialization. One important note was that bureaucratic structure requires a certain level of self-denial, which is difficult to maintain. In developing a bureaucratic structure, Etzioni identifies the detail used by Weber in constructing a rational structure. Those details are as follows:

1. Any organization identified to have authorized functions should be constrained be specific rules;
2. Systematic division of labor with the appropriate amount of control and power over those divisions is essential;

3. A hierarchy exist;
4. Any rules may be technical in nature;
5. Members of the administrative or executive pool should be separated from ownership of the corporation;
6. Workers should be flexible for various types of allocation and re-allocation; and
7. All organizational decisions are documented for records.

This is typical for industrial businesses.

Etzioni speaks of a Utilitarian organization. Utilitarian organizations support concepts of industrial or corporate organizations. In some regard, they align to his explanation of Scientific Management structures. He describes the compliance nature of such an organization to be in all three power structures based on subcategories he developed. The subcategories are blue-collar, white-collar and professional. All denoting various skill level jobs defined in industry. Other organizations discussed are normative and dual, where normative organizations demonstrate normative power and dual organizations have dual power structures controlling the organization. Etzioni reminds us that these types of organizations may exist in a primary and secondary format based on the organizational needs.

An important observation by Etzioni is that in the functioning of organizations specific goals determine the structure of the groupings and therefore the organization. In describing the affect goals have on an organization he makes a great point in perceiving that goals may be, the driver of the organization or the organization may drive the goals. This process demonstrates the motivation of the organization. In his discussion, he speaks to the development of organizational goals and references the displacement of goals. He provides insights as to how some goals are set. He believes that employee's goals should be separate from organizational goals. In his descriptions, organizational goals are the desired future state of the company. He builds no relationship to the employee's goals. The structure of the organization lends efficiencies to achieving organization goals. As well, he relates effectiveness of the organization structure to the realizations of specific organization goals. Eztioni suggest using a goal-model approach or a system model approach in measuring organizational success. The goal-model approach is only measured by the realization of the organizational goals in effective methods. The system model approach completes a comparative analysis of the entire system of organizations that exist in a corporation and measure the systems success of goal achievement. This process shows the relationship between organizations. Within the system-model approach, there are two sub-layers of models. These are survival and effectiveness models. The survival model exists because it achieved its organizational goals. The effectiveness model defines the interrelationships that exist in the system model. The effectiveness models compare the effectiveness of the independent organization and relate the results as an overall effectiveness.

Another area of interest was the controls of charisma; Etzioni defines this power as a source of compliance for an organization also. Yet, charisma places constraints on an organization because it gives the individual high personal power. In analyzing charisma three new forms of organizations develop, they are T, R and L. This terms developed establish the distribution of charisma within the organization. T-structure definition is charisma distribution is at the top layer or positions of the organization. L-structure definition is charisma distribution is at the line position of the organization. This is within a hierarchal system such as the Catholic Church. The R-structure definition is charisma distribution is at the rank level. The R-structure supports limits to the distribution of charisma. He relates these forms of charisma to the effectiveness of the organization and power structure. Etzioni highlights that organizations with L-structures have more problems based on level of commitments within and around the line of control. This produces a level of dysfunction within the organization. The L-structure supports that engagement of and opinion of all at the specific level.

Etzioni does not discuss in detail the development within the structures. With Etzioni's establishment of goals and power system used to monitor and control the hierarchy effective organizational development methods are producible. By aligning to the various concepts of compliance, as well, organizations productivity establishment is possible also.

Hall begins with common definitions of organizations. Using terms created by Weber, Bernard, and Marx, Hall assembles the definition of an organization as Etzion's defines it. Social units purposed fully constructed to meet a specific goal. Hall then further describes organizations based on the outcome of the organization, which focuses the organization on goals. By reviewing system constraints that affect organizations, Hall communicates an organization definition in three parts, which are structure, goals, and results. "An organization is a collectivity with a relatively identifiable boundary, a normative order (rules), ranks of authority (hierarchy), communications systems and membership coordinating systems (procedures); this collectivity exists on a relatively continuous basis, in an environment, and engages in activities that are usually related to a set of goals; the activities have outcomes for organizational members, for the organization itself, and for society" (Hall, 2002). Hall identifies organizations as living beings. He states that organizations are long living organisms that develop certain patterns and processes based on the members. His major distinction is organizations have lifecycles. Meaning there is a beginning and an end to them through the process of time. The organization cycles through the process by the concepts of change. With the change of goals, there may be a change in the organization. Hall believes to achieve change an organization must exist. Hall uses three terms to describe his analysis of organizations. They are taxonomy, typology, and classification. In simplified concepts, typology explains standard organizational structure based on the organizational functions. He identifies organizations as complex systems, which have various classifications. Hall's analysis of classifications is a secondary level analysis that allows the reader to understand organizational function. Hall uses reference to Etzioni's compliance analysis for examples of classification. With this, they identified nine additional categories for organizational structures. Hall also uses references to Mintzberg in understanding deliberate typologies that have multifaceted methods for developing organizational structures. Mintzberg's approach further supports Hall's belief that organizations are not only typological structures but have defined classifications or taxonomy. In the development of this body of knowledge Hall creates organization taxonomy, which embraces class levels from the study of over seventy-five organizations. Initially, this approach deemed that it did not provide the structure analysis needed, yet, many additional theorists agree taxonomy is the best approach. Hall continued to review variable requirements to segment class levels and appropriate taxonomy approaches.

Hall determined that organizational structures are "the distributions, along various lines, of people among social positions that influence the role relations among these people (Hall, 2002)." This process does not define labor task or hierarchies. Implication of those processes dictates that there are lines drawn along task division and responsibility. Hall describes organizational structures as having three basic functions:

1. Produce outcomes in achieving goals
2. Minimization and regulate the effect of individual variations
3. Define power influence, decision making, and organizational requirements completed

Hall also determined that within these structures there are many lower level structures. This aligns to the class level taxonomy of organizations. These structures within a structure have the same central functions that the outer layers have. Many though may not roll-up to the higher-level goals. Hall uses the work of many others to describe the various types of structural forms. Using the work of Weber, Burns, and Stalker, Hall identifies the bureaucracy, mechanical, and organic systems. Each structural form defines its hierarchical systems and control networks to align with the organizational needed. Hall's central point of his body of work is to evaluate the complexity of the organizations. Hall believes the complexity of the organizations contributes to every layer of the organization. The affects relate to the behavior of the individuals at all levels in the organization, the structural form of the organization, internal procedures of the organization, and the environmental condition of the organization. Individuals entering an organization recognize the complexity based on the division of labor and management, as well as, power structure. The issues arise in the understanding of the subunits and control mechanisms. Hall examines additional variables of complexity that relate to structural layout. They are horizontal differentiation, vertical/hierarchical differentiation, and geographical dispersion. Horizontal's definition is the number of job divisions in the organization. Vertical/hierarchical's definition is the deepest number of levels in one division. Geographical is the number of divisions spread out in multiple cities, regions, and countries. These differential alignments contribute to varying layers of the organization when it comes to power and control. This reflection further concentrates the complexity levels of an organization. The differential structure relates to the end item product concerning its complexity. The individual layer of these differentials highlights the focus on goals, the group dynamics and life cycle of products. In any of these, organizational structures methods for conflict resolution assist in the success or failure of the organizations. If there are, no methods the life cycle of any group is shorten based on system resolutions.

Gareth Morgan's approach is very different from previously discusses theorist. Morgan (2006) attempts assist the reader in developing methods for understanding organizational life. The process is to provide a metaphoric view of organizational creation, development, and survival. Morgan demonstrates that for many years inanimate object references where used to structure and develop organization. One of the first metaphors used was organizations are machines. Morgan stated, "When we approach metaphor in this way we see that our simple premise that all theory is metaphor has far-reaching consequences (2006)". The basis for such a statement forces us to understand the differences, as well as, the alignments. In the analyzing the organizational needs and structure what areas have we not considered that might affect the achievement of goals. If theory is metaphor then Morgan contends that no single theory provides a complete view based on the differences not described. Morgan then proceeds to describe various metaphors that insinuate certain concepts about the nature of the organization. Morgan does not describe for the reader any methods for job design or hierarchical structure rather he uses the metaphor implementation to develop perspectives. This perspective aids management in understanding organizational success and failures. It also provides insight in developing methods to strengthen the organization.

In reviewing the idea of organizational life, the organizational structure contributes to defining the metaphors used by Morgan. Morgan describes organizations as instruments to realize an end state. Morgan stated, "This is reflected in the origins of the word *organization*, which derives from the Greek *organon*, meaning a tool or instrument (2006)." He then attests to the alignment of this definition with the expectation to achieve goals etc. The first metaphor example Morgan describes is that of a bureaucratic organization. The bureaucratic organization term's creation was in 1920's with Weber's contribution. The effectivity and efficiency is the purpose for bureaucratic organizations. All job sections and control are well defined. Bureaucratic organization references machine or mechanical organization. He examines classic approaches Classical Management Theory and Scientific Management. Highlighting major areas of concern such as staff line, unity of command, train the worker, and etc. The purpose is to show the parallels to that of standard machinery. Morgan scrutinizes the alignments and contradictions of the machine metaphor to these systems. Morgan emphasizes the constraints of this type of organization. Things such as:

1. These forms may have problems with aligning to a changing environment
2. The organization may develops routine and needless methods for activities
3. The independent worker internal goals affect the organizations in the achievement of it goals
4. Many view lower level tier of workers as dispensable

These are some of the negatives to having systems structure in bureaucratic formats. These descriptions provide management with determining effects of organizational life. One might see these issues in dysfunctional organizations.

Morgan continues to develop additional metaphors with emphasizes on the strengths and limitations of various organizational types. The analysis of strengths reflects on the successes of the organization with reference to working environment, employee involvement/behavior, and flexibility of the organization. The limitations discussed reflect on aspects that constrain the organization in fore-filling its definition of success. He calls attention to the affects such that meaningful strategies developed move the organization to a position of success.

Organisms is a metaphor he uses to describe an organization that functions as an open system, procedurally adapts to changing environments, maintains awareness of it position in the life cycle, develops the organization for additional needs and reviews of evolution of the organization. Morgan identifies additional organization types that function in what he terms a mechanistic-organic format. The definition of such is an organization that maintains a bureaucratic structure, yet functions based on the business need. He uses the findings of Mintzberg to further this discussion. These organizations are machine bureaucracy, divisionalized form, professional bureaucracy, simple structure, and adhocracy. Using driving factors for these organizations specifies their relationship to management. These driving factors vary in relation to effectivity, product, environment or efficiency. The structure of the organization i.e. hierarchies aid the organization in process implementation.

Additional metaphors are "Learning Organizations" are Brains, Social Reality are Culture Organizations, Organizations as system of government, Organizations as psychic prisons, Organizations as flux and transformation, and Organizations as instruments of domination. In each of these, he demonstrates the application of them within the organization and the impact on the organization. He does not state that one process fits all. There are many factors that have to be considered in analysis and implementing these types of environments. Each has very different effects on the worker within the organization. He provides additional theoretical procedures for moving the organization from one metaphor to another.

3) *Organization Processes*

The internal processes of the organization assist in the controlling the organizations. Gibson *et.l* also reflects on internal organizational processes. Process developments for accurate and comprehensive communication are important to the success of an organization. Gibson et.l provides a communication model that follows the standards developed by the early work of Clause Shannon, Warren Weaver and Wilbur Schramm. Gibson *et.l* includes an area on cultural differences in communication. He identifies differences in contextual words used, personal spacing and communication timing. Gibson *et.l* states differences in polychronic and monochronic cultures. Gibson *et.l* describes cultural that use a polychronic process in communication, in which the individual does many things at one time. The monochronic process definition requires the manager to complete one task at a time. Directional communication discussed basis are on the organizational structure. In today's organization, there are many forms of communication to use. The organization should determine what method works best for them.

Another organization process is the decision making process. Gibson *et.l* identifies two types of decisions. Those are programmed and non-programmed decisions. Each may have program effects. Programmed decisions generally are decisions made on a daily basis. Whereas the non-programmed decisions have, more long term affects on the corporation. In either case, standard decision making procedures enable the organization to review and understand actions required by the decisions. The decision process generally begins with the corporate goals. As goal monitoring takes place, should there be any issues, solution reviews and alternative deliverables provide management with pathways to success. Additional factors contribute to the success of developing good solutions to problems. These factors are values, personality, and propensity to risk. In the process of making a decision and completing evaluations, the individual's behaviors in the context of values reflect in the various schools of thought. The ethical responsibility, in relationship to economics and legal obligations are the foundations of values in making good decisions. The personalities of the individual concerning the person's attitude and beliefs contribute to the individual's internal desires, which are the drivers in the person's personality. Then there is the risk avoidance level within the individual and the affects that avoidance has on decisions relates to the individual's internal fears. In the process of making decisions an individual should not fear making the decision or completing something that maybe outside of their normal process. Risk avoidance may be an idea killer for the future of the corporation. There is also cognitive dissonance, which is what some term the "regret theory". It is the times in decision making with the individual's develop anxieties about the decisions made. Gibson *et.l* notes that these behaviors are individual but application to groups is a consideration. In an effort to limit some of these affects, Gibson *et.l* highlights techniques to formulate decision making in groups. Techniques such as Brainstorming, Delphi Process, and Nominal Group Techniques (NGT) move the group to creating ideas and making decisions. Brainstorming is creativity encouragement to generate ideas is the focus, without criticism. The Delphi Process allows individuals within the groups to anonymously judge the ideas generated. NGT is a face-to-face meeting that mathematically pools the outcome by voting. There is very little communication in a NGT process.

In organizational development, Gibson *et.l* emphasizes themes from Argyris and Knowles in developing systems that unfreeze old learning, move the person to new learning, and refreeze new learning. He encourages the use of change agents as interventionist, either internal or external agents. Gibson *et.l* underlines reasoning for resistance to change and methods to limiting that resistance. Gibson *et.l* provides a seven-step model for managing organizational change that reviews the following: forces of change be-it environmental or internal, review of performance deliverables, diagnosis of any problems or issues, determine interventions as needed, what are the inhibitors, implement actions to solve problems, and final evaluations. In the process of determining interventions additional approach implementations, such as analysis of various entities in behavior, structural, or technology need consideration.

In all cases it Gibson *et.l* underscores that need to have a learning organization. Gibson *et.l* describes ten factors that facilitate a learning organization. These factors are scanning the environment, performance issues, metrics, experimental philosophy, transparency, education, operational variety, multiple advocates, and engaged leaders and role models. Each contribute to the embracing a learning organization. With management understanding these perspectives, a corporation develops an open environment, where inclusivity is the norm.

As the complexity of organizations grows, Etzioni directs his attention to the need for organizations to be compliant. He then defines compliance as "both to a relation in which an actor behaves in accordance with a directive supported by another actor's power, and to the orientation of the subordinated actor to the power applied" (1971). Etzioni believes the power within the structured organizations determines the success of goal achievement, efficiency and effectivity. He goes on to describe three types of power. Power's definition is the workers capability to sway another to complete the worker's commands or any other decisions the worker engages. These powers are coercive, remunerative, and normative. Generally, power dictation follows the structure of the organization. The need for power may be greater if the complexity of the organizations is larger, than the management structure is able to monitor. Coercive power's definition is power defined by the application. Meaning how the power is applied. In many cases, this power is an intimidating process that threatens the workers. Please note the published date of the information. In today's organizations, such tactics are not allowed in the corporate work environment. This does not mean that they do not exist. Human relations organization procedural requirements and the government overseers prohibit usage of such power. Remunerative power is the control of materials and rewards through salaries, bonuses, etc. Normative power is as stated by Etzioni, "the allocation and manipulation of symbolic rewards and deprivations through employment of leaders, manipulation of mass media, allocation of esteem and prestige symbols, administration of ritual, and influence over the distribution of acceptance and positive response. The normative power has a negative influence, as well as a positive influence. The normative power demonstrations occur more in a vertical fashion for organizations. This means that lower level people use manipulative methods to receive symbolic awards. This focus on power aligns to Etzioni's concepts of compliance organizations to the power structure. The Coercive organizations use certain methods of power on the lower level workers and induce high levels of alienation between people within the organization and leadership.

In the process of compliance organization, there are three types of organizational goals. They are economic, culture and order goals. Each goal is from a different viewpoint. The economic goal provides measures on commodities and services for outside customers. The culture goal provides the development of environments that create and preserve other symbolic concepts and their applications. It builds commitment to these concepts during creation. The order goal provides control over workers that are deviant concerning the social norms of the organization. This goal separates them from the social unit to prevent additional deviant actions. This goal is negative. It provides a measure of acts prevented by the organizations rather than the production of goods. The relationship of organizational goals and compliance lay in the type of power maintained in the system. The coercive organization has order goals. The utilitarian organization has economic goals. The normative organization has cultural goals. In general, all systems may have a combination of the three goal types. For example in a factory, you would have goals based on economics due to the products you develop. You would also have goals relating to defects and rework, which are order goals, as well as, goals for establishing a specific type of environment for workers, i.e. open and honest (cultural).

In addition to goals process, decision-making processes are vital to the organization. During the writing of Etzion's body of work the decision making theories were non-organizational theories. During his time, these processes dealt with individual decision making regardless of status or position. Generally, speaking decision-making basis was mathematical analysis and logical reasoning. It described the steps to take to make a decision. Etzioni references the on-going study of individual processing for making decisions. He does not discuss in detail due to the lack of data it seems.

Etzioni (1971) elaborates more on concepts of effectiveness and efficiencies. Etzioni describes specific goal types and effective complaint organizations. Etzioni states that economic goals are more effective with the use of remuneration power rather than coercion or normative. Within the organization, the use of remuneration power provides motivation to the worker to accomplish the task to complete production. Production activities provide rational structures where reward and money distribution basis are within the established goals. Normative and coercion powers exist in these organizations but are not as effective in achieving the set goals unless there is a level of legitimate power established requiring commitment from the worker. In some instances, economic goals in organizations with normative power are highly effective but this results stems from the organization being a service focus organization. These organizations are fire fighters and police officers for example.

Cultural goals produce effective output in normative power structures. The level of commitment to the organization and the goal drive the importance. A certain level of charisma is required in developing effectiveness in these organizations. These organizations are churches etc. Identification, with the organization representatives influences the attainment of goals. Coercion powers limit identification with the organization such that cultural goals are not successful and the organization is ineffective.

In the case of order goals, effective compliance develops from coercive power rather than the others. By using remunerative power, the establishment of negative consequences is the driver. In establishments such as prisons, this process is highly ineffective based on the history of the individual involved in the organizations. Normative powers are also ineffective because it is difficult to maintain compliance in an order-oriented environment.

In reviewing structures for compliance, Etzioni moves the reader into various methods of leadership. Based on the structures hierarchy Etzioni establishes a term such as elites, which he denotes as the individual that has power in the organization. He separates the concept of elites into two forms. Elite's labels are officers or leaders. Officer have power base on position, where leaders have normative power. This is also the establishment of formal leaders and informal leaders. On occasions some individuals may have both types of power position and normative. Yet, in the case of an informal leader, the power structure defined is coercion. The basis is their methods for influencing various individuals within the organization. The importance of the elite status revolves around methods for goal achievement and organization effectiveness. Etzioni also states that collaboration is a process that occurs when an informal leader holds the values and belief of the formal leaders without having position.

Hall begins his discussion of process with the suggesting that organizations need formalized processes. The formalization of processes contributes to the success of an organization. Hall acknowledged formalization as a key variable to for individuals within the organization. The formalization of processes develops a preprogrammed behavior for individuals. It removes some of the individual discretion. It assists the organization in functioning. Hall makes a great connection centralization of power and formalization. The relationship identifies that there may be less formalization of rules if the when the decision making power is central to the organization. The more formal processes require less centralization of power. The thought seems to lend itself to individuals following the strict rules developed by the organization.

Hall further explains additional third level variables related to formalization, centralization and complexity. These variables are context and design. Each relate to the structural forms of the organization. Hall defines context as "Contextual explanations include organizational size, technology, internal culture, the environment, and national cultural factors" (2002). Based on how the organization functions dictates the context within the organization. These contextual factors may be controlled be the organization or may not be. They can have external contributors. In the area of design, the central focus is the achievement of goals and the effectivity of the organization.

In discussing the factors that contribute to the development of an organization and the impact complexity, centralization and formalization, Hall describes the effect of processes on the organization. The understandings of power within the organization provide the desired outcomes. Hall describes power as an interdependent relationship where there is dependency on one another. This identifies with the structure layout wherein the manager needs the employee to have a product. He states that power has two aspects to reflect on, where power is a preformed. Power is either used or not. He also establishes that power and authority differ in that power relates to force or coercion. Authority implies deferment of judgment by the receiver. Within authority, there is no force. Hall uses definitions developed by Weber (1947). Power typology is rational-legal, charismatic, traditional and influence. Where ration-legal focuses on today's organizational formal structure, and aligns itself to the hierarchy of the system. Charismatic power focuses on the individual's personal characteristics. Traditional is the monarch system established in various environments. The final is influence where position is not a factor but the persuasive nature of an individual provides them with power. He further divides power into a second layer of factors, these being bases and source. Power bases definition is what the individual controls such that they have an effect on individual behavior. Power source relates to whether the individual has the ability to reward and coerce individuals. These power factors align to organization because in that each usage provides a specific outcome. He even mentions the existence of cliques and coalitions in organizations that may affect control and power structures. Powers also influence conflict processes. Hall states the conflict internal to organizations relates to power based on the methods used to resolve these conflicts. Conflict situations evolve from many components of an organization. Based on the power structure the conflict may be functional, unit, or hierarchical. Which flows to the next layer of differential understanding, individual, group, or organizational, that may require a specific procedure for resolution.

Other areas of study, by Hall, are leadership, communication and decision-making. These factors relate to the formalization of organizational processes. These processes assist in the effectivity of the organization. To further, the concept of organizational lifecycles Hall discusses the impact of change to an organization. I introduce this here due to the fact the Hall specifies organizational procedures that may be implemented. Based on Hall's perspective of change, the survival of the organization and the avoidance of death is the greatest challenge to an organization. Change in an organization relates to external pressures and internal goals. The need to remain marketed and contributing to society are factors of these pressures. They relate to a need to change the organizational goals. Hall describes organizations in constant flux and requires individuals to learn new things and unlearn old things. In the mist of such change, Hall states the individual are a prospective cause of inertia. Organizational policy may contribute to maintaining that inertia.

In the change process Hall's definition, better describes the lifecycle of an organization. Hall states that there is a birth and founding in organizations. This stage is the "creation of an operating entity that acquires inputs from suppliers and provides outputs to a given public" (Delacroix and Carroll, 1983:276: Hall, 2002). Founding aligns to biological analogy, which developed from a later study of organizations. The next stage is transformation, where after birth the organization begins to alter itself for various reasons. Hall states that all organizations transform once created. The basis is the newness of the organizations, as well as, the small size. Small organizations are subject to external and internal pressures that cause them to change. Hall (p187-188) uses references to the work of McKelvey and Aldrich in ecological theory, which speaks to the survival of organizations. The principles created by McKelvey and Aldrich define the operation in ecological process. Principle "1" relates to variations in the organization that may have purpose or limited vision. Principle "2" relates to degree of variations, which allows the organization to acquire the appropriate resources for survival. In some events, the variations may cause the failure or the success of the organization based on the level of resources obtained. Principle "3" relates to preservation of resources and dissemination of those same resources. In the process of retention, the need for knowledge transfer and skills maintance is major factor to the continued success for the organization. Principle "4" relates to the continued fight to survive. The fight for survival basis is on the need for to resources fore-fill organization goals, established by strategic objectives. If the needs are unmet, the organization dies. Death is the final stage of the lifecycle. Hall states that death takes place in stages also. The stages are the following:

1. Blindness to signals of demise
2. Recognition of signals but no change takes place
3. Recognition of signals yet inappropriate response are in acted
4. Catastrophe from the inappropriate responses
5. Dissolve the organization

The stage is a referred to a downward spiral, by Hall. Hall mentions that death may not be caused by a failure of the organization. Hall makes a point to identify that innovation within the organization may halt the stages of death in an organization.

In the process of the lifecycle Hall identifies additional factors in the birth and founding of organizations. Hall highlights the relationship between the environment and internal relationships that contribute to the success of an organization. Within the environment education of individuals and skill base effect the development of the organization. Even the technical opportunities effect the internal workings development of the organization also. Additional factors are environment dimensions and analytical dimensions. Hall reminds us that these dimensions effect, the structure and form of the organization. The effects relate to additional business needs or managerial control. The environmental dimensions are technical needs, legal requirements, political position and power, economic flows, demographic make-up of the community, ecological resources needs, and cultural stance. In the area of analytical, the dimensions are environmental depth and growth requirements, environment differentials, environmental strength and weakness, environmental spacing between sites and set-ups, environmental domain and market strength, and finally the interconnections of these environmental factors.

Other areas that Hall covers demonstrate a detail understanding of organizational modeling and creation. He describes many varying levels of relationships and connections that embrace the complexity involved in creating organizations. The introduction of a lifecycle allows theorist to analyze the varying levels and layers of the organization for successful implementations.

It was interesting to evaluate each of theorists, in many ways they were similar in their approach. There were four major areas reviewed to complete a compare and contrast. These areas were organizational structures approaches, behavior analysis, power structure, and organization lifecycles. These areas reflect a network of relationships in the organizational system.

The introduction of the charisma structure aligns to the influence of power. Etzioni's use of this concept improves visibility within the hierarchy. The influence of control and power are major factors organizational structures. Hall, Gibson et.l, Etzioni, and Morgan discuss power within the organization. They highlight that power may be distributed at all levels of the organization. The lowest level of power is within the group and/or team. In this instance an individual, influences the teams in various directions. As we move up the hierarchies system, the power is more positions based. The individual in position makes decision based on their views. The importance of power to any organization relates to obtaining organizational goals and objectives. In early stages of organizations controls, power structures and hierarchical distributions dictated the line of command. Etzioni even refers to the miss use of power in organizations. The power corruptation contributes to the organizational failures. Etzioni describes an instance where fear of losing power caused some leadership to manipulate the power they held and move people into intimidating positions. Decisions process definitions beit vertical or horizontal focus the power and the use of control. Etzioni charisma inclusion speaks to political influences in decision making within the organization. Centralization and decentralization of power broadens the definition of power and political controls. Hall also uses Bacharach and Lawler to further describes power sources within the organization. These sources are structural position, charisma, expertise, and opportunity. Morgan's discussion aims to bring attention mainly to the failures of power and control. Morgan demonstrates that concept in the metaphor Psychic Prison, which details the use of groupthink to maintain individual control. Morgan provides a view that power held in many organizations is positional. Morgan references that individuals in positions of power contribute to the type of organizational system your corporation has. With the spread of power, influence decision-making identification at all levels aids in managing the power distribution in the organization. In many cases, the decision-making executed at the lower levels has more success. The flow of information and communication seems to be easier at the lower levels. The moves to higher levels in the organization communication processes are more difficult to control. Filtration of information as it flows up the hierarchy takes place. Most high-level managers have little to no data as to what happens at the lower levels. There are occasions when this is not the case, yet most organizational systems develop communication processes to flow data up and down the hierarchy.

Hall introduced the concept of a lifecycle for organizations. In this, he uses many methods of recognizing when the organization changes or requires a change. The difficulty of change in an organizational structure drives directly to the where the organization is in their lifecycle. In any of these cases the product developed by the may not be a factor in the growth or death of the organization. Hall moves to make the point that factors such as technology, environment and market positioning contribute to the organization's lifecycle. The resistances to change with the environmental factors produce even more pressure on the organizational system. Hall also describes the death cycle of the organizations, in which leadership indentifies the need for change. Hall details the process of death cycles and how new organizations develop from this process. Morgan realizes that there is an organizational cycle that all go through. In the process of philosophically describing organizations, Morgan introduces the implementation of moving from one type of metaphoric organization to another. By identifying the strengths and weakness of the each analogy, he aids organizational structure in creating the best organization for their product system and market needs.

Each theorist provided interesting perspectives to the internal and external relationships developed by the organization. By analyzing of organizational structures, organizational effectiveness, and theory, principle theorist will understand product, environment, and individual development in successful organizations.

b) Organizational Concepts

In corporations, organizational structures are the definitions of the companies. Gibson *et.l*, Hall, Morgan and Etzioni structure their findings on hierarchical bureaucratic systems with additional information in job structure, resource needs, and product development. The systems evolution over the years contributes to concepts Hall highlights in his writings. Hall (2002) directs us to five models in analyzing an organization. As stated earlier each has individual purposes based on the corporation and environment needs. The five types are population-ecology model, resource-dependence model, rational-contingency model, transaction-cost model, and institutional model.

Each model contributes to portions of Morgan's analogies of organizations, yet is unidentified within the same methodology. The population-ecology model develops from the environmental needs. The drivers in the development of such an organization are what Hall refers to as niches. Niches are holes in the environment that requires some form of support in which an organization provides. The focus is the appropriate fit for the environment. Goals are not the focus of this type of organization. The resource-dependence model structure moves decision-making within the organization. The environment drives the resource-dependence model also. There is no consideration to goals and objectives. Within resource-dependence models, decisions align to the strategic focus of the organization. This reviews the relationships with the external environments. Rational-contingency models align to goals and objectives. The set strategy centers on decision-making that reinforces the achievement of goals. The leadership and group focus are achievement strategic objectives. The organizational culture basis is the attitude of the organization. Transactional-cost model evolved from economics. The transactional-cost basis establishes the market relationship of payment for goods and services. In the process of trade transaction, development defined the free-market. Over the past twenty to thirty years this process complexities have grown. The final is institutional model, which is an isolated morphing system. There is no rational reasoning in its development. The structural base drivers are external and internal pressures, which take the shape of other organizations.

Each theorist referenced within this breadth contributed to extending organizational concepts. Etzioni begin his process in the earlier 1900's. Etzioni contributed to Hall's, Gibson's *et.l*, and Morgan's research. Etzioni based his research on discoveries of Weber and etc. As many theorist of that age psychological behavior practices was not a part of his work. In most of this process, that exclusion is a weakness. Based on the fact in the twenty first century many corporations identify more that Maslow hierarchies of needs is applicable. Etzioni did evaluate the negative side of organizations, yet during his dominion, there were few opportunities to understand the phenomena. The issues were not deemed to have been behavioral based. During his time, the contributor to bad behavior was economic. Etzioni description of various organizational structures such as that of the R and T structures for charisma developed an interesting view of power. Etzioni provided insight to the influences of such formats. This process builds on the topology concepts of power. This added insight is a strength to organizational studies.

Morgan's concentrates on the organizational structure and the functioning of that structure. His process directs organizational structural analysis for implementations. In several of his analogies, Morgan centers on the individual. Morgan identifies the limitations in overlaying organizational processes such as communication and decision-making. This based on the organizational structure and hierarchies. In comparing the organizational structures with metaphoric symbols, Morgan is able to dissect the organizational weakness and strengths. The metaphoric symbols allow Morgan to build individual behaviors relationships with the hierarchy of the system.

Each of these systems is the foundations for many corporate organizations toady. In addition, in many cases based on external pressures to remain an organization the system may morph. The implementations of such system, Morgan emphasizes.

c) *Development of Organization*

In most cases, the concept of development focuses on skill training and job assignments, yet there are other areas of development required for a successful organization. The organizational lifecycle demand organization growth and learning. This goes beyond the task level improvements but includes environmental needs. Survival is the purpose.

Most organizations frequently analyze the environment and competitors, yet alittle may change in how they do business. This builds the direction of the company and contributes to the underline strategy. Areas such as technology, governance, and market needs force a review of the structure of the organization. The need to have a learning organization enhances the output of that organization. Morgan describes a learning organization that functions as a brain. In most of his analogy, Morgan focuses on double-loop learning. Suggesting this process should take the place of single-loop learning. Morgan also emphasizes the need to have management support in expanding the learning. Morgan believed that learning should take place at all levels. Morgan suggests that similar to cybernetics certain capacities contribute to building a learning organization. These items are:

- Analyze the external and internal environments for major variances
- Establish an environment that encourages questions, transformations, and test system customary processes and the status quo
- Provide opportunity for processes to develop
- Embrace management such that double-loop learning takes place rather than the traditional processes

These actions give the organization opportunities to remove some bureaucracy. In any organization, change should become the norm and flexibility with that process allows the organization to develop with the surrounding environment. The involvement of double-loop learning aids the organization in removing many individual defensive routines and highlights internal conflict that may exist in the management structure. Morgan (2006) proposes using the Holographic process in developing the brain. The Holographic process has five principles to develop this environment. The Holographic process aligns to a self-organized organization. The five principles are:

1. Emulate the entire organization in smaller sections
2. Redundant processes in the smaller sections
3. External influences align to the internal system complexities
4. Maintain few requirements

5. Openness to learning

This process opens the system to flexibility concerning the impacts of the external environment. It provides the system with prototype environments. This method enables staffing needs to be interchangeable. The formulation of small teams building complete systems internal to that team allows close loop solutions faster.

Gibson *et.l* discusses learning but in a very different capacity. He describes the need to have a leadership process that flows down to the nonprofessional worker. The commitment and purpose of the learning communicated on all levels of the organization. Gibson *et.l* suggests that certain philosophies should inhabit the management structure and align to corporate business goals and objectives.

II. Learning in the Corporate Environment

There are varying degrees of learning that takes place in corporate America. In the previous section, the learning focuses on the learning of management. The process implementation should take affect on all levels. Gibson's *et.l* approach aligns to the system implementation of change. A changing organization embraces learning. Gibson *et.l* focuses on concepts of freezing and unfreezing the learning. This approach is applicable at the management level as well as the non-professional. The process requires that workers unfreeze old learning, which attributes to the learning new things and refreezing the new learning. Gibson *et.l* even suggests using punishment in instance to remove the old behavior. The fear is that the new training will be lost when the new behavior is unimplemented.

Many in the corporate environment desire to have learning organizations. This goes beyond the standard process learning that takes place. The movement is that the organization continuously learns in an effort to improve internal processes. Gibson *et.l* refers to learning principles used by various authors of six sigma principles, developing organizational principles, and maintaining completive environment principles. Gibson's *et.l* (2009, pp506) perspective list is as follows:"

1. Scanning the environment	Interest in external happening and in the nature of one's environment. Valuing the processes of awareness and data generation. Curious about what is "out there" as opposed to "inhere".
2. Performance issues	Share perception of a gap between actual and desired state of performance. Disconfirming feedback interrupts a string of successes. Performance shortfalls are seen as opportunities for learning
3. Metrics	Spend effort to define and measure key factors; strive for specific, quantifiable measures; discourse over metrics is seen as a learning activity
4. Experimental philosophy	Support for trying new things; curiosity about how things work; ability to "play" with things. Small failures are encouraged, not punished. See changes in work processes, policies, and structure as a continuous series of graded tryouts
5. Transparency	Accessibility of information, relatively open boundaries. Opportunities to observe others; problems/errors are shared, not hidden; debate and conflict are acceptable
6. Education	On-going commitment to education at all levels; support for growth and development of members
7. Operational variety	Variety exist in response modes, procedures, systems; significant diversity in personnel. Pluralistic rather than monolithic definition of valued internal capabilities
8. Multiple advocates	Top-down and bottom-up initiatives are possible; multiple advocates and gatekeepers exist

9.	Engaged leaders and role models	Leadership at significant levels articulates vision and is very actively engaged in its actualization; takes ongoing steps to implement visions; hands-on" involvement in educational and other implementation steps

Table 1 Gibson *et.l* (2009,pp506)

This list provides a guideline for corporation to review where they are in this process. He goes on to provide assistance in what actions leadership should take in this process. Many of these concepts focus on manager developing the vision and implementation plan for the organization.

Summary

In summary, all of the theorist contribute to the body of knowledge in different formats. There are many similarities in the area of organizational structure development and approaches. The contrast in behavior analysis for all theorist included in this breath demonstrate evolution of the science. Gibson's *et.l* contribution to the development of individual behavior analysis created a personal understanding of the individuals within the organization. Hall's introduction of organizational lifecycles provides industry with methods of survival in the corporate environment. Etzioni adds insight to the development of complex organization. Etzioni's comparison of various types of organization moves structure analysis and organization development to deeper understanding of power processes. Morgan's review of the organization structures and effectiveness allows the organizations to development environments conducive to the success of the organization. Morgan's analysis broadens Etzioni's comparison to system strengths and weaknesses.

CHAPTER 2

Organizations of Today

Corporate environments have multiple structured organizations. The corporate environment demands businesses create some type of organizational structure. The analysis of organizations requires an acknowledgement of organizational development models and learning models in relationship to functional and dysfunctional systems with organization. I will also compare and contrast how organizational development philosophies contribute to the development of present learning organizational models. The final discussion compares the affects of functional and dysfunctional organizations with a growing and diverse workforce. The depth shall be a review of articles written in the last five years. The articles reviewed detail some of the latest research and analysis of Gibson *et.l* and other theorist. The documented application of these models details how organizational development is anchored in the area of change theory. There are articles annotations summarizing each and selecting a key quote.

I. *Literary Discussion*

   a) *Organization Analysis*

     1) *Definition of organization*

The organizational development and learning models align to change models. Organizations are evolving daily to accommodate the changing needs of the customer. The role of the organization in providing products and services, I will define organizations as a set of people grouped to achieve a specific goal. The definition is broad enough to encompass a variety of approaches to implementing learning systems in organizations. Based on the organization's needs a learning system maybe an imperative to the survival of the organization, which a specific approach highlighted by both Gibson *et.l* and Hall. There may be a social need, which created the organization as Etzioni describes. Yet, in either situation, the development of an organization became a necessity to meet a desired goal. Organizations provide methods of control for any group in non-profit or profit settings. In the development of organizations the concepts of hierarchies establishes a defined context to align job assignments and boundaries of control.

2) *Levels/Hierarchies of organization*

The structure of an organization varies based on industry and profit desires. There are standard mechanical approaches to organizational structures that exist from the industrial age. These structures provided layering control for the organizations. Decisions evolve from the organization's internal process. The processes are either centralized or decentralized. These approaches of centralization or decentralization align to the power structure requirements of the organization. The power structure may be a visible layering to the organization or invisible layering. All paths should lead to achieving the organizational goals.

Hall discussion of typologies provides a simple outline for organizational structures. The listings of the five distinct types of organization structures are simple structure, machine bureaucracy, professional bureaucracy, divisionalized form, and adhocracy structures. Each aligns to some system process of decisions and power. The system in which they exist dictates the need for layering and flow of information. Generally, simple, machine and professional bureaucracy's power center is the president of the company. In this position, he or she may delegate decisions and obtain feedback. This is a centralized approach based on the geographical location of the elements of the organization. Hall further describes organizations as building structures. Aligning the beam structure to that of the organization, although not an exact mirror to the development of one but detailed enough to understand the highest point to the lower flooring. Hall emphasis the two additional factors that affect organizational structure such as contextual and design. The contextual concepts of an organization affect the physical realm of the organization. The design affects the strategic layout of jobs and assignments. This added depth to the acknowledgment by Covey (2007), "The global economy is experiencing an economic tsunami that most organizations are hardly aware of. Just 20 years ago, manual labor represented 70 to 80 percent of the value added goods and services. Today, it's knowledge work that represents 70 to 80 percent, while manual labor is more like 20 or 30 percent." In the process of job designs and assignments, the measures taken to improve the hierarchal structure are few in numbers. In Morgan's review of organizations a reflection of the environment are components used to determine the structure of the organization. Morgan's argument that the typical hierarchical layout many not be the best fit for the company's goals and the achievement of these goals. While the process of manual labor has decreased over the last 20 year, the methods used for control and power should evolve. This also point back to the analogies Morgan made in having prison type structures or structures that are more organic. Covey (2007) states that having skilled people are important to the organizations and should move to learning environments. The importance of intellectual capital is a lifeline to the success of companies. Covey refers to the work of Thomas Stewart, in stating, "Intellectual capital is intellectual material knowledge, information, intellectual property, experience- that can be put to use to create wealth. It is collective brainpower. It's hard to identify and harder still to deploy effectively. But once you find and exploit it you win." The use of intellectual properties may halt based on the structure of jobs and the culture of the company. Once again that moves us back to the analogies developed by Morgan determine the strengths and weakness of various organizational structures. The need for many may be in evolution to different formats that remove some of the controlling parameters and aligns the powers bodies to the intellectual property structures. Covey states the top down control structure from the industrial age usage in the knowledge environment is a problem. The introduction of new generations in the work environment brings new challenges to the old structure. The move to globalizations requires the acknowledgement of such changes and challenges.

3) Analysis of Organization

Organizational development generally focuses on the changing of the organization to meet some need. The concept of functioning and dysfunctional organizations emphasizes that organizations have behavioral characteristics that may contribute to their success and failure. The functioning organization exhibits actions of achieving its objectives with little negative impact to the working environments and structures. A dysfunctional organization is the opposite concerning environmental impacts, yet the organization may still meet its objectives. A dysfunctional organization is an organization that does not use standard means of control and communication. The dysfunctional organization will have dissatisfied employees at all levels. Fleet (2006) describes dysfunctional organizations are ultimately practicing dysfunctional behavior. Dysfunctional behavior intends to harm the organization, individual employees, and stakeholders. Dysfunctional behavior is antisocial behavior. Dysfunctional behaviors become a system norm and a part of the central culture. The dysfunction becomes a problem when behaviors cause expenditure of profits. The profit loss occurs through re-work, overtime pay, unachievable processes, and etc. Each of these areas point to issues happening within the organization and team during execution is considered external symptoms of dysfunction. These dysfunctions are organizational stresses, organizational anxiety, and destructive behavioral norms. In many case Fleet (2006) refers to these behaviors as "the dark side of organizational behavior", which affect the organization negatively.

Gibson *et.l* specifically highlights three areas that generally require development. These areas are structurally, behaviorally, and technically. Based on the organizational goal all three areas may be affected. The need is to evaluate the company needs and the organizational outputs. In most cases companies use methods such as Porter's Five or "Strength, Weakness, Opportunity, and Threats" (SWOT), to determine market strategies to improve various company objectives, these process may affect the organization's structure, the behavior of employees, and the technical interfaces necessary to achieve tactical objectives. Gibson *et.l* then provides a seven-step model that allows management to understand the forces that require a change in the corporation. The seven-steps within Gibson's *et.l* process align to the philosophies of those business methods. The seven steps are understanding forces of change; what are your desired performance requirements; evaluate the problem prohibiting this performance; determine the required action or intervention; what are the constraints internal that may prohibit the change; develop a method of implementation; and examine your results. There may be a need to loop back through the process of implementation if the constraints change. In processing through the forces that may cause the change, Gibson *et.l* provides low level mapping to the three areas of development, structure, behavior, and technical. In reviewing external forces Gibson *et.l*, suggest that technologies, market and resources are the areas impacted. The internal forces are behavioral and processes. These forces may affect the performance of the organization, teams, or individuals. In completing an organizational analysis, business objectives can develop dysfunction in an organization. The relationship between goals and individuals can contribute to behavioral discourse, power structural problems, and charisma clashes.

The affect on the structure emphasizes the work of Morgan in determining the weakness and strengths of various organizational structures. By understanding the product and environmental needs of employees, reviewing the organizational structure examples provided by Morgan, systems improvements might be available. An article highlighted below documents the use of prototyping in organizational change and behavioral analysis. The article is by Peter Coughlan. The prototype process allows the organization to implement their changes in a controlled group for analysis and review. These type of implementation models for structural change assist in Gibson's *et.l* process of execution. The driving factor though to understand the current system analysis, through performance measures for effectivity, cost, production, and etc. In determining cause and effect, the article presented by Kohler in evaluation of symptoms the implementing of a comprehensive stress management program (CSMP) may be possible. In any event, the analysis of the organization is a requirement for successful

b) *Organization Behaviors*

The challenges of globalization focus into the internal makeup of the organization. All organizations are groups and teams made up of individuals with one central goal or objective. In the much of Gibson's *et.l* concepts, the behavior of such elements dictates the success or failure of an organization. Gibson's *et.l* references the work of Kurt Lewin, who proposed that behaviors in algorithmic terms is $B = f(I,E)$ where behavior is a function of the individual and the environment factors. In any case, the behavior of the individual is a factor in the behavior of the group or team, which ultimately feeds into the organization. The lowest common denominator is the individual.

1) Individual

Gibson *et.l* (2009) reinforces the fact that individuals respond based on all phases of their environments. These phases include any point in the life of the individual. Yet within the area of the job behavior it is the generally agreed to by the following (Gibson *et.l* 2009,pp 93):

1. Behavior is caused.
2. Behavior is goal directed.
3. Behavior that can be observed is measurable.
4. Behavior that's not directly observable is also important in accomplishing goals.
5. Behavior is motivated.

Where anything a person does contributes to their behavioral definition. Management's understanding of the individual abilities and skills, aids in the placement of that individual. In this regard, management has to be cognate of behaviors. Gibson *et.l* describes the difference in ability and skill, where ability aligns to the mental capacity of the individual and skill focuses on the physical skill of the individual. In many cases, the manager must be aware of such attributes of the individual. The mental abilities of the individual demonstrate their cognitive learning and development. In a knowledge industry, this area is of most value. The mental capability speaks directly to the wealth of the company. Managements emotional intelligence level is a technique used to assist managers in this area. In the physical arena, the individual's specific external factors contribute to the job designed for that individual. The next layers of understanding in the individual relm are gender, racial and cultural. All of these are underlined driver to the individual's behavior. These notional attributes contribute to the internal and external perception of the individual. The perception of an individual develops from their cognitive processing. The cognitive process has environment contributors to its development. All of which affect the individual's behaviors in various surroundings.

The dysfunction of these behaviors may evolve from various areas of mental ability, mental skill, or physical ability. In the process of developing a product, the impact occurs throughout the system flow. When an employee is unable mentally to complete a task, stress and anxiety will occur. This reaction develops into additional behaviors of not completing workflows to meet schedule dates or management's request. The result is re-work and delay further down the workflow. This moves negative behaviors up the hierarchy when decisions are made. Gibson's *et.l* point that there are five phases to job behavior, which can be affected based on environmental factors aligns to the introduction of what I will term dysfunctional job behaviors. In an article by Fleet, concepts analyzing personality patterns provides some insight to the causes of the dysfunctional behavior on an individual level. In most organizational development environments personality test are common practices. Fleet highlights details of Type A behavior patterns and Type B behavior that contribute to behavioral problems within the organization. Fleet describes the Type A personality as one that displays aggression and is involved in conflict problems within the organization. In addition, Fleet stated, "Thus, genetic and biological factors, personality, values, experiences, and motives are all likely to affect an individual's disposition to display dysfunctional behavior." In the analysis of organizational behavior, the individual behavior adds to the foundation of the process.

2) *Group and Team*

Most would define groups and teams as similar entities, yet their functions within an organization are very different. Each has a particular purpose in the life of the organization. Gibson *et.l* defines groups as "collections of individuals in which behavior and/or performance of one member is influenced by behavior and/or performance of other members." In determining the behavior of a group, we must first determine the type of group. There are formal groups and informal groups. Formal groups have position in the hierarchy within the organization. The formal group may have goals that compliement the overall organization's goal. These enities report up to higher levels within the organization and may have the same discipline. Many groups have the same job design and task. The informal group is causal in nature. The informal group may not report up to any level in the organization nor have the same organizational goals. The informal group may be a social group with an entirely different purpose. The behavior of a formal group meets certain organization needs in developing products. Groups can learn and develop. Gibson *et.l* highlights that groups go through development phases such as storming and norming. These phases demonstrate the maturity level of the group. Each phase reflects on the behavior of the group members. Throughout this process, the group formulates such concepts as structure, hierarchy and roles within the group. Gibson *et.l* also refers to Punctuated Equilibrium Model. The PEM model presents three phases that groups go through in the process of development. The development of group norms becomes the static behavior of the group. These norms may be negative or position. The behavior of the group stemmed from the leadership of the group. In examination leadership assist in the development of a cohesive nature. The group develops into a supportive entity. This phenomenon is referred to as group think. Gibson et.l describes groupthink, within highly cohesive groups, as Irving Janis stated a "deterioration of mental efficiency, reality testing, and moral judgment in the interest of group solidarity." Gibson et.l states "groupthink is a cohesive group's desire for agreement interferes with the group's consideration of alternative solutions. The outcome of groupthink can have a negative impact if the leadership of the group has additional conflicts within.

Gibson *et.l* defines teams as more specific task groups. There are mature groups with specific skills and goals. Within the team the hierarchy is defines as well as the roles of the individuals. Team creation may be short lived once the goal or objective is achieved. The formation of teams may enhance productivity based on the structure of the team. The affect of a team for organizations is the flattening of the organization. Teams exist in various formats from virtual or centralized. Teams can also have a certain amount of autonomy based on the length of time of existence. Teams allow for more flexibility in decision-making and embrace diversity within the work force. There is the threat of groupthink even in the team. Groupthink offsets happens with the inclusion of diverse skills and people.

The behavior of both teams and groups depend on the individuals that make up the group. Conflict arises in both settings. This contributes to dysfunction of such entities. As the group matures, the group norms become the culture of the group. This process may take place within a team but the lifecycle of the team dictates the longevity of the process, yet in the event the same team members become involved in the same team structure for various external goals the establishment of a group norm/culture happens. The leadership of the team establishes the heart beat of the team. If the leadership is negative and dictative the response of the team may be dysfunctional behavior. Dysfunctional behavior is less likely to continue when the team dissolves. The culture of the company develops as the central culture of the group, yet this process may not be the affect on the team or group. Power and charisma within the group or team takes a dominate role in the function of the team. The types of power displayed are expert and referent. The makeup of teams concerning experts lends itself to internal conflicts when there are many experts within the same skill on the team. The conflict resides in role allocation within the team. The conflict is demonstrated when a team expert's placement is not of that individual's expectation. In such a situation, the concept of coercion occurs to move the team a specific direction. The result can be a dysfunctional team that is not meeting their goals and objectives. The phenomena may take place within a group also. On occasion, a team may have multiple individuals with referent power or charisma. This individual's ability to move people based on what Gibson *et.l* calls magnetic personality moves other individuals to agree with their framing of concepts. When this process happens, the group may be split and counterproductive to the accomplishment of goals. The result in either case is dysfunction. Dysfunctional groups and teams become dysfunctional organizations.

c) *Organization Development*

1) *Learning*

Organizational development's fundamental purpose revolves around the corporate needs and pressures from external environments. Gibson *et.l* states that external factors from market, technology, and resources require the internal organization to evolve. As part of this process Hall's reference to organizational lifecycles, force the corporation to scan the environment for organizational survival. The development of the organization is key contributor to the corporate goals. Organizational development is the development of the individuals within the organization. The growth and evolution of these individuals supplies the organization with the skills necessary for success.

Organizational development happens in areas such as individual skills, behavior, and processes. The alignment of these areas allows the corporation to extract value from the underlying system. Each of these areas provides the internal system greater opportunity in accomplishing company goals. Organizational development is related to change models. Gibson's *et.l* Seven-step model described in section (3) Analysis of Organizations assists in determining what the mode of action should be. In most cases upper level management in many organizations desire to have learning and action learning organizations. The purpose of having such organizations places the corporation in environments of flexibility. The agility of an organization to change when the need presents itself is an overwhelmingly valuable characteristic. Generally, learning as defined by Gibson *et.l* is the process of behavioral changes based on continuous practice.

An action learning organization, as stated by Donnenberg and Loo (2004), is a learning system focused on the individual. Although it is, a defined system structured to focus on the organization as well as the individual. The framework Donnenberg and Loo (2004) used centered concepts of scripting, lean think, and mindsets. Action learning according to various evaluations is an organizational change method accomplished through individual changes. Therefore, as the individual develops personal areas of change the organizational affects are soon to follow. This relationship may not take place on every occasion. Yet, there is value in the process of action learning. Donnenberg *et.l* demonstrates in his article a defined framework created in building the relationships between the organization and the individual. His first applicable concept is scripting. In the development of the cognitive system, scripting allows an individual to evaluate the situation and action demonstrated without being the decision maker. The process enhances communication and action analysis. It assists in breaking cognitive processing causing the individual to think about the actions taking place. Donnenberg *et.l* references a list phases the action-learning participants should take based in evolving to a solution from J.R. Mercer. They are the following phases:

- "Make a review of one's problem situation"
- "Present this review to the action learning group"
- "Propose an outline of the way one thinks a problem should be tackled"
- "Present this outline to the group"
- "Discussion"
- "Implement the resulting solution in one's work setting"

An important process to understand is the usage of the individual's cognitive scripts and behavior scripts. Donnenberg's *et.l* distinctions between to two are the actions the individual take are behavioral scripts the process of selecting a behavior is the cognitive script. Therefore, in action learning Donnenberg *et.l* states "behavior scripts are observed cognitive scripts". The desire is to change the behavior scripts through the phases described in the production of new cognitive scripts. These develop into what Donnenberg *et.l* termed protoscripts, which become the institutionalized method for implementing action learning.

In the area of lean thinking, Donnenberg *et.l* highlights studies J. P. Womack, D.T. Jones, and J. Seddon (2003) and the concepts focus on the following factors:

- "Creation of customer value"
- "Rearrangement of the entire value chain (and the corresponding work processes)"
- "'Flow' improvement, so that the goods moving through and the activities taking place be coordinated such that as little interruption or delay as possible occurs"
- "Production is only pulled be customer demands"
- "Continuous improvement"

Lean thinking is the entry to concepts like action learning organizations. In developing the protoscripts it is important to note there can be a change in the mindset of the individual. Moving into actions demonstrated within the organization.

Basic learning takes place at various levels of an organization. The development of employees can align to specific goals of the organization. In developing a learning organization, the focus is evolution. The organization makes efforts for continuous improvements. The need of that improvement and expected outcome should be defined. Based on the external force management should equip the organization to handle the change. Management learning and employee learning requires motivation. In most cases management rewards management for learning new skills and behavior changes, yet, for general employees learning is defined differently. The corporate needs for learning rest in the corporation's survival. Learning on all levels and rewards for that learning on all levels institutionalizes the belief that learning has an importance. The increase in this area relates to the increase in knowledge value within an organization. Change models described affect employee's relationship with the product and therefore increase specific types of learning. Yet, there are other forms of learning. They are social and operant conditioning. Social learning involves cognitive process, demonstrating different behaviors based on environmental factors, according to Gibson *et.l*. Social learning may or may not have positive impacts do to the fact that the basis for interaction is the individual surrounding environment. The Pygmalion effect of social learning, as described by Gibson *et.l,* relates positive expectations to learning and/or performance. The operant conditioning defined by Gibson *et.l* is the learning that occurs based on some consequence of behavior. This type of learning aligns more to an environment of punishment rather than reward.

In Morgan's example that organizations are like brains, therefore having full capability to learn and develop is in contrast to some concepts of Herbert Simon. According to Morgan, Simon's description of human learning lie in the rational processing of the individual. Morgan highlights Simon concept that based on the institutionalization of human rationality the about for detail in-depth decision-making is hindered. In recent studies decision-making tool development for data collection and organizing aids industries in the decision-making process. Yet, single loop learning, the foundation of human boundaries, delay advancements in continuous learning. Morgan describes Argyris's concepts of double loop learning by illustrating the questioning of system norms for applicability and value. Double loop learning without technical systems is useful in the implementation of learning systems. In all of this process, it is thought that individuals evolve from data collected and data loop backs to the organization. The looping back of data and change in actions to accommodate information constitutes learning for the organization. Morgan makes a strong statement that in any part f the process the boundaries that exist in the capability of learning and decision-making lies in the human. This comment focuses on the limited intelligence of individuals, therefore justifying the limited intelligence of the organization. Morgan embraces theory developed by Argyris in stating that information blockages occur in defensive routines human create during decision-making processes. Morgan strongly suggests that information technology and data analysis is an aid in creating a learning environment. Models developed using Cybernetics system demonstrates the ability of information evolution. The concepts fundamentally embrace theories of communication and self-regulation. This process imposes a self-regulating organization in which detected errors implement real time solutions. This would be a system of constant organizational development. The second part of that process is the human system that interacts with the system. To develop a learning environment Morgan (2006, pp87) suggests the following as implemented by the cybernetics environment:

- "Scan and anticipate change in the wider environment to detect significant variations
- "Develop an ability to question, challenge, and change operating norms and assumptions"
- "Allow an appropriate strategic direction and pattern of organization to emerge"
- "Evolve designs that allow them to become skilled in the art of double loop learning, to avoid getting trapped in single loop processes, especially those created by traditional management control systems and the defensive routines of organizational members.

Morgan encourages organization to adopt environments where change is the norm. In the embracing this changing concept early indicators of process needs causes a behavior of pro-activity rather than reactive. Morgan states that learning organizations are successful when emphasizes placed on environmental truths cause analysis for action rather than inactive processing. This process develops an innovative culture that competes with evolving industries. Morgan emphasizes, "a learning organization actually change the environment in which it exists." Morgan focuses on the importance of organizations uplifting an environment that creates opportunity for discussion that may have conflicting values.

Dysfunctional organizations seem to have individual issues with defensive routines that prohibit a learning environment. The actions of protectism and fear decrease the activity of double loop learning. The dysfunction of the organization can be attributed to skill level, roles, or behaviors. To determine the complexity of the issue recommendations to scan the internal environment and encourage double loop learning.

Learning takes place in many ways. The organization must be open to understanding the vision and customer. The organizational development process may focus centrally on skill. The solution to such implementations aligns to school and classes. Yet, when the focus emerges from external drives the relationship to learning is different. It may require open modeling of communication and decision-making to move individuals. The fundamental process lies in conceptually understanding your industry and the needs of your corporation.

2) *Goal and Productivity*

Organizational goals and objectives drive the corporation in America. There is a relationship between organizations developing to meet goals. The development may align to a product process or behavior modification on the part of the employee. In any event, the overall objective in organization development from a goal perspective is productivity and efficiency. Productivity improvements align to organizational development in a similar way such as goals. In organizational development the goal, creation and maintenance may take place at all levels of the organization. Most corporations seek to align lower level goals to that of management. Gibson *et.l* states that by detail goal setting individuals sub sequentially perform at higher rates, based on the work of Edwin Locke. Goal setting removes subconscious bias and subjectivity concerning management review and employee understanding.

Organization development aids in the achievement of corporate goals on an individual level. Gibson *et.l* states that goal setting can be a motivator when used appropriately. In the development of the individual contributions to the goal setting and goal achievement, organizational development of learning assist in that process. The summary of actions may increase total productivity. Learning ultimately becomes a priority of the organization.

Morgan's suggestion of using Japanese philosophies in Total Quality Management in relaxing the need to setting goals at higher levels the organization develops method and models of double loop learning. The idea of goal setting in a hierarchical system focused on controlling the system emphasizes single loop learning. Goal setting maybe a constraint to the system concerning innovation and creativity at the employee level, the achievement of goals can skew the appearance of errors within the system.

In any organization, environmental factor consideration provides the corporation with mapping strategies for instituting organizational development structures. An analysis of system needs and desired outcomes with regard of external factors, allows individuals and manager to implement correct systems of innovation. The overall desire is to have an organization that is self-analyzing, self-diagnosing and self-correcting.

d) *Interactive and involved Leadership*

Included in all of these concepts are assumptions of leadership involvement. A requirement for organizational development and functional organizations is inclusive leadership. The level of commitment from the leadership is dictative to the level of success of any implementation. A functional organization is one in which social behavior of the employee at all levels reflect some level of normalcy. The actions taken by the employee within the organization are not counterproductive to the advancement of company initiative and organizational processes. There is a high degree employee satisfaction. Functional organizations have efficiencies, effectivity, and performance higher than peers do in the same industry. Organizational learning applies to management as well as subordinates.

Gibson *et.l* defines leadership in four realms; they are either job-centered or employee-centered and initiating structure or consideration. Additional factors contribute to determine which direction the leadership may follow. Gibson *et.l* defines job-centered as one closely monitors the work of the employee. Employee-centered is one monitor in a broader fashion and allows the employee to have some self-rule. Initiating structure is one that is more goal and results oriented in that they define the complete job task and responsibilities required. The consideration type demonstrates a higher level of open communication and sharing with the employee. Effective leadership exhibits multiple facets of these processes. Gibson *et.l* reveals the concept of situational leadership and models that define these processes. The "Contingency Leadership Model" suggests that group output basis depends on leadership style and a favorable environment for the situation. This model centers around situational awareness of the leadership and the application of a particular leadership style, such as relationship or task oriented. Gibson *et.l* describes the "Path-Goal Model" where referent methods of power applied to the employee-manager relationship changing the viewpoint of the employee in a positive way concerning their goals, performance, and career development. The next model is "Hersey-Blanchard Situational Leadership Model", in which the leadership style used is dictated by the maturity level of the employee and the situation. In examining the maturity level of the individual, some attainment measure of readiness is achievable. The final model is "Leader-Member Exchange Theory (LMX)" where leaders are thought to form grouping systems for employees and based on that grouping dictates their personal interaction with the employee. The model reflects an inclusive and exclusion process the leader has concerning the groups that developed. As stated earlier leadership's commitment and participation in the development of employees is an important factor to whether an organization is functional or dysfunctional.

The purpose for examining leadership models is to build the relationship of employee performance to the leadership style. Each model demonstrates different methods for communication and interacting with the employee. Gibson *et.l* further details the fact that studies show there is strong relationship between leadership behaviors that affect subordinate levels of satisfaction. In addition, the employee's performance affected leadership's focus on concerns and behavior-performance connections. These relationship factors contribute to organizational functioning and dysfunction.

An article reviewed demonstrates the impact leadership has on organizational performance. Goldman (2006) describes an environment where the leadership reacted emotionally to all situations. The emotional response varied from negative to positive. Due to the fluxions of emotions, the business unit began to perform poorly. It was determined leadership within the organization caused employee satisfaction to decease and ultimately employee output decreased. The leadership label was "Highly Toxic". The leadership used more of the LMX model in attempting to achieve company goals. The highly toxic leadership developed a very dysfunctional working environment for employees. In this case, the leadership discovered there was a medical issue causing the fluxions and with medication the work environment change. Leadership took additional training. Change was positive in that employee satisfaction and performance output increased.

In the article written by Fleet *et.l* the actions of management, contribute to the dysfunction of the organizational cultures. Fleet *et.l* describes dysfunctional organizations as "A dysfunctional organization culture is defined as one that constrains or limits individual and group-level capabilities and/or that actually encourages and rewards mediocre individual and group-level performance. Fleet *et.l* states "Leaders, however, are perhaps the most powerful determinant of organization culture." The organizational culture is greatly influenced by the leadership. This culture dictates that behavior of its leaders. The relationship to leadership demonstrated in constraining tactics or rewarding processes highlights developing functional or dysfunctional organizations. In situational analysis, the LMX model or any model that may aligns to far to the left or right of job-centered and individual-centered leadership styles contribute the creation of a dysfunctional organization. Fleet *et al.* also bad leaders frequently have dysfunctional organizations and rarely meet organizational goals. Higher-level management dysfunction cause lower level groups un-effectively complete job assignments. According to Fleet *et al.*, dysfunction can flow down the hierarchy of the organization there making the entire corporation dysfunctional. Fleet *et al.* states due to the lack of interpersonal skills and legitimate power leadership nay become abusive in tactics used to manage people. The negative social behaviors exhibited by leadership once again are toxic to the organization. In relationship to learning organizations and organizational development these individual have determined that skill development in change, communication, time management, conflict resolution, and stress are unimportant to the achievement of company goals.

As describe in the article by Balthazard *et.l* dysfunctional organizations display certain characteristics and behaviors. Baltharzard *et.l* aligns dysfunction to low levels of performance and efficiency. Key factors are the organizational norms and behaviors at an individual level and an organizational–unit level. Baltharzard *et al.* describes the implementation of the Organizational Culture Inventory (OCI) survey. The survey is a statistical method of analysis used for consulting and change processes within the organizations. Baltharzard *et al.* uses the survey to measure standard behaviors within the organization related to three formats of organizational cultures. The three formats are "constructive, passive/defensive, and aggressive/defensive." Baltharzard *et al.* measures behavioral standards by examining two areas. The first area being the consideration for people verse task and the second area being anticipations of certain actions aligned to the higher levels of Maslow's pyramid verses maintaining lower level needs. Baltharzard's *et al.* uses the survey based on the behavioral standards because of the objective relationship to beliefs and values. The thought is that norms and anticipations have more influence in the daily activities of the individual. The value of such a survey is demonstrated in the results present. Functional organizations desire to have a constructive environment supportive of good behavioral norms. The survey provided data to identify dysfunctional behavior that could affect the organization.

Leadership impacts to organizational culture also affect the anxiety levels within an organization. Baruch *et al.* describes a clinical implementation on organization phenomena. The implications suggest that organizational stress level control lie in leadership styles, where leadership style definitions are illustrated above in this document. Baruch *et al.* suggest that such stresses are preventable creating happier employees. The outcome is a functional organization. Baruch's *et al.* went as far as describing physical issues that may occur in the event such anxieties appear in the organization. Baruch *et al.* introduces an organizational model developed to analysis the progression and administration of anxiety within the organization. The analysis of external drives of the organization is common practice. The introduction of this model provides a behavior analysis based on internal symptoms. The continual injections of stress from external and internal forces evolve from lack of social influence and little management interaction. Baruch *et al.* states based on the underline requirement of trust within the organization a defined communication process should be implemented. The presence of such processes provides portals to management and employee for bidirectional communication. The importance of such mechanism is highlighted in Baruch *et al.* process model flow. This model then focuses on coping mechanism that would also need to be in place. Mechanisms created maybe the catalyst to developing new environmental changes implementations.

The overall objective is to have functional organizations. The need for leadership to be open and communicative relative to a diverse work environment is a central goal. The concept of dysfunctional organizations grows daily. This may be in part to the variety of new entities involved in the organization today. During the industry age one solution implementation was the norm. Yet, that model does not apply anymore. We are in the knowledge and information age of technology. New environments require new strategies. Throughout this section leadership styles and contributions to dysfunctional organizations were discussed. The implementation of new methodologies and models were also introduced. In combination the need to continuously improve is proven to be a corporate success measure.

e) *Next Generation of Organizations*

Today there are four different generations within the organization. The need to integrate these environments is in contrast to methodologies used ten years ago. Construction of new models that incorporate the varying personalities will move organizational structure development to the next generation. New modeling structures of the system contribute to building successful relationship between management and employee. Innovative processing of data and open systems assist in successful implementations of collaborative organizations. Understanding the product development and organizational needs provides valuable input to developing learning organizations with functional structures and work environments.

II. Summary

Organizational development is a branched system. Each branch being another layer to the complexity of the organization requiring corporate change for success, OD is thought to be the remedy for whatever ails the organization. Most corporations have business goals in developing successful OD entities. With the evolving market for OD models and systems, one would believe that real solutions exist. In reviewing the existing concepts of organizational structures and the bureaucratic hierarchy, little evolution has occurred. There are expanding theories, which Morgan introduced, yet very few entities make use of them. There are two general types of organizations, organic and mechanical. These structure function using the same general methods of control and power. Each has conceptually introduced various internal processes to aid in the success of the organization.

The market environment changes daily due to innovations. The organizations must be flexible to engage in this new world. With the external stress that businesses see the need for behavior alignment is crucial. Developing learning environments that understand constant change are new strategic goals for many. Aligning the leadership to handle any and all situations using leadership model are the norm. In the same processes, there is little consideration for the human aspect of the system. The models developed for change and leadership dictate instructions to complete or work flows to institute. The reflective mapping of human nature and human behavior seems to be standardized. The development of dysfunctional organizations is due to people void of social interaction on a meaningful level. The implementation of behavioral analysis systems and limiting single loop learning establish healthy organizations.

CHAPTER 3

Developing a Workable Model

The Application section is developed to implement the concepts discussed. The development of a model aids in understanding organizations, recognize problems and issues, and implement step system for improvement. The model structure is to analyze organizations on all levels. The first level analyzed is the individual level. The next level reviewed are groups and teams, which overall makes up the organization. Leadership analysis makes up a portion of this process. The model developed shall introduce methods for changing a dysfunctional organization.

BACKGROUND

Recently, Organizational Development departments are major parts of the hierarchy. Organizational Development existence became required in organizational goals and objectives. With the introduction of diverse workforces, organizations are in need of change. Additional management models used to assist leadership in handling a variety of situations. The evolutions of organizational change management processes and models have overwhelmed the market. Organizational surveys on employee satisfaction and management 360° degree surveys continue to be popular. In many OD and organizational theory documentation, little data exist in behavior and dysfunctional organizations. Organizations that are unable to meet their company goals or implement company initiatives start to ponder boundaries that prohibit their evolution. The leadership models of today rarely affect the areas that cause the dysfunction. In many organizational change initiatives where technology changes and people have to adapt or the organizational structure changes. Organizational structure changes evolve from unmet goals or low productivity on the part of the employee. The models developed focus on managing people yet the data shown that most organizational environments have chaos from two sources. One being the employee themselves and the other leadership's methods implemented.

ORGANIZATION DIAGNOSIS AND STRATEGIC ACTIONS

The Application section discusses a strategic model providing organizations with the ability to evaluate their internal compass and make better employee decisions. The intended audience is any organizational development group or corporate leadership. Presently, there is no preliminary implementation environment. This structure provides an implementable model for organizational development of dysfunctional organizations and creates learning organizations.

The intention of this Application is to build a course that develops emotional intelligence to the new manager. The theoretical frameworks suggesting this Application are those of Etzioni (1964, 1975), Gibson *et al.* (1976, 2009), Hall (2002), and Morgan (1997). The following section will address organizational analysis strategic models for developing organizations. The analyze successes and failure of model implementation. This section will also provide a learning model for organizations with diverse groups.

I. *Organizational Needs*

Organizations have life cycles similar to that of products. In the process of innovation, organizations have to be willing to change and grow. The life cycle of a product is need or niche, requirements, design, development, manufacture, consumption, and death. Once the community consumption of a product reaches a certain level or a new product, evolution happens the death of the first product is following. The lifecycle of an organization is similar. The organization meets a need, has requirements, is designed, developed, has life, and dies. In the process of life for the organization, goal achievement and corporate success are the lifeblood of the system. The environment of today requires much more for sustainment. The corporations of today have continual evolution and innovation requirements. It is not enough to meet your company goals for profit. The corporation has to scan the environment and be aware of changes looming. The corporation has to be flexible enough accommodate the changes to the internal and external environments.

Changes for a corporation have many drivers from market share to lack of resources. In the mist of all of this change, leadership of the organizations has to respond and react accordingly. In some cases, these reactions have negative effects on the lower levels of the organization. Depending on the organization, the outcome can kill the organization and move the corporation to ruin. For that reason, I shall use various works of leading theorist to aid in strategic model development, which will assist in the assessing of an organization and methods to improve the health of the organization. This is monitoring the organization for functional environments and dysfunctional environments, which contribute to the health of the organizations.

II. *Change Drivers*

Most companies have strategic plans developed ten or twenty years in advance. Corporations attempt to drive the market in the direction that is best for their industry. Corporations attempt to anticipate the moves of the market if they are unable to drive the market. The winners are those that are successful in driving the market. For example, Apple and the IPhone changed human interactions with cell phones. Many external factors though can alter those expectations in seconds. The tools used to analyze and understand market movement are Strengths, Weakness, Opportunities, and Threats (SWOT), as well as Porter's Force Five. The development of business strategies is an unintended subject matter. The purpose, as stated is with the use of the fore mentioned tools, is how we minimize a negative effect on the organization with the changes in strategy and external environments. Most corporations implement intense leadership training and process improvements. In addition, focus on innovation and product improvements become key initiatives. Where is the consideration for the nonprofessional worker? What is the impact on achieving company goals? Gibson's *et al.* seven-step model for change provides a meaning method for implementing change to the organization regardless what the driver for the change is. In the following sections, I will use this model and Gibson's *et al.* concept of three change approaches. The intent is to expand and integrate the models with corporate drives.

In any event, external drivers are environmental and out of the control of the corporation. Elements considered as part of this group are economic market, evolutional technology, or a decrease in available resources. Internal drivers are elements that affect external outcomes. They are elements, which the corporation own and evolve internally. These elements generally have more affect on the individual. Each implementation is ultimately a change implementation. The results are dependent on the process and methods used to implement the change.

In Etzioni's (1964) statement about organizational goals, we have to be aware of the slave master process that takes place. In evaluating external drivers, goals structure aligns to the competitive review of the market. I would argue there are two sets of goals established that drive the companies. The first set relates to external drivers. Those external drivers are profit, loss and market share. The impact of those goals presents themselves as strategic business goals. Internal goal labeling are initiatives. The affect of such goals on the organization moves me to describe the organizational models segmented by external and internal factors. To align with my objective I discuss goals as the master of the organizations based on corporations aggressive pursuits to be listed as the number one corporate within their industry. The purpose is to develop efficient and effective processes.

1) Change Models

Change models are major components to organizational development. The process of developing and organization is simply to move i.e. change the organization from one means of execution to another. In reviewing the subject matter, I discovered Burke's (1992) detail on implementing multiple change models. Each contained three fundamental steps. Step

1 is unfreezing the present process functioning. The method imposes the concept of stopping the present behavior. Step 2 is to move the individuals to using the new process and implant a new system concept. This method advances the individual to new actions and cognitive behavior. The last step is refreezing. The purpose is to freeze the new behavior as the natural response.

Burke introduces models from Lewin (1958); Schein (1987); Lippitt, Watson, and Westley (1958); and a generic model for organizational change. Each model demonstrated the standard three steps. Burke illustrated Lewin's process as a looping method that continually collected data to determine the level change produced. In the looping, if the freezing and refreezing process need to re-implementation then such actions happened. Burke communicated that Schein on the other hand expanded Lewin's process by establishing lower tier level unfreezing and re-freezing concepts. For example, in the unfreezing stage Burke stated Schein proposed using tactics such as inducing guilty, highlighting the overall need, or introducing some form of fear. Burke then analyzed Lippitt *et al.* extended the method of change by highlighting the five phases of Lippitt's *et al.*, which are: (Burke, 1992, pp59)

1. "Development of a need for change (Lewin's unfreezing)"
2. "Establishment of a change relationship"
3. "Working toward change (moving)"
4. "Generalization and stabilization of change (refreeze)"
5. "Achieving a terminal relationship"

Establishing the position of the change agent as part of this process was Lippitt's *et al* belief. Burke describes a generic model evolved from these models. The generic model has the following elements:

1. External professional with human behavioral expertise
2. Survey and organizational data is collect prior to the arrival of the professional such that appropriate action is implemented
3. Consult with the system or impacted organization for agreement and collective analysis.
4. Apply proposed change to the system
5. Institute the change as the formal process

Each model expanded the base concepts of change models. Burke then introduces a model that anticipates behavior and performance outcomes. Burke therefore incorporates a cause and effect process within the change process. According to Burke, the environmental forces are the central reasons for organizational change and development. Burke highlights key variables that influence organizational change. The secondary levels of variables have an impact and build on the relationships established by the higher-level variables. The higher-level variables are strategy, leadership and culture. The related variables are structure, management practices, and systems. Burke stated that in planning change implementation requires alignment with strategy and leadership behavior. To better communication, the relationships established by Burke, I refer the elements as objects. Burke illustrates that the object "Leadership" have relationships to "Mission and strategy", "Individual and organization performance", "External environment", and "Organizations culture", which are higher level objects. The next layers of relationships exist for the lower level variables are:

Second level:

- Management practices
- Structure
- Systems

Third level:

- Work Unit climate
- Task Requirements and individual skills/abilities
- Individual needs and values
- Motivation

Each the above listed objects are related to "Individual and organizational performance", which builds on the higher-level objects related to leadership. The Leadership relationship creates, what Burke considers, transformational dynamics. Transformational dynamics are actions caused by interfaces with environmental factors. The next layer of objects cause transactional dynamics, which are actions created in a reciprocal process. Because of the action in one area there is a reciprocal effect in another area.

The final model review was the "Seven-step Model for the Management of Change". Gibson's *et al.* model format is in the Breadth and Depth. This model is similar to the concepts Burke introduced. The over arching difference from Burke, yet very much like the others is a guided step process. In Burke's model due to the relational aspect of the model, you could be at in phase in the process at anytime. There is no sequence of events. The models both highlight the need to understand external forces, as well as the present performance of the individuals and organization. Both Gibson *et al.* and Burke considered some framework of the organization's culture. Gibson *et al.* alludes to it in acknowledging internal constraints. An area to review for the Gibson *et al.* model was technology; within Burke's review, he segregated the system as an independent factor. Technology, at an external level was an independent factor, yet in the process of intervention, it was an area for review and application.

In the change model I developed, which will be discussed later, I attempted to combine the philosophies of both Gibson *et al.* and Burke. I based this on the fact that both provided you with in-depth detail in analyzing the present processes of the organizational structure. Feedback loops for cause and affect demonstrated the complete model. As shown in Burke's model the change process is always in two phases transformation and transactional. The overall forces of change beit internal or external drive either transformation and transactional.

2) *Constraints to Implementations*

Within all of these processes, people are the core resources. The success and failure of implementation lie heavily in the hands of the people involved. In the initial models of Lewin should there be a portion of the old teaching remain frozen in the learning, the process would start at step one. The facilitator goes back to the unfreeze process and move the individual to the new learning. The process would continue until the change seemed fully implemented. In all of the additional models the concepts of failure to implementation was not part of the process. In each model, the change looped back for implementation until the achievement of success. Action learning as the formal process to loop through the change process until the new behavior is frozen. As part of the action learning new plan development recalibrated unfreeze and freeze process. In the Schein's model additional techniques make the unfreeze portion of the cyclic and emotionally driven. In the following steps of Schein's model, similar techniques emphasize the emotional reactions to structure the change and freeze the new behavior. Similar implementation methods in Lippitt's *et al.* demonstrate the feedback loop for unfreezing and freezing new behaviors. The Burke methods cyclic loop for successful implementation continues until the new behaviors exist. In each of these cases, some analysis of change needs and implementation strategies aid in the process of change. In the Burke and Gibson *et al.* models the data collected about the culture, performance and system increase the chances for successful implementations. A specific difference in the model of Gibson *et al.* and Burke is that Gibson *et al.* acknowledges that there may be constraint preventing the change. Some constraint factors in Gibson's *et al.* model are leadership and organizational culture. As stated in the depth leaderships culture has a strong impact on the implementation of organizational change.

To understand organizational development implementations I looked at Argyris and Schon's (1996) details of organizational learning. Argyris *et al.* focus of the failure of organizational implementations aligns to defensive routines. Argyris emphasizes the organizational learning systems. As part of this process the organizational communication environment provides a baseline understanding norms and culture. The communication process can be an inhibitor or contributors to successful organizational development i.e. change implementations. This relationship exists in the behavior of world individuals and openness to questions within the organization. Argyris stated "By the "behavioral world" of the organization, we mean that qualities, meanings, and feelings that habitually condition patterns of interaction among individuals within the organization in such a way as to affect organizational inquiry – for example, the degree to which patterns of interaction are friendly or hostile, intimate or distant, open or closed, flexible or rigid, competitive or cooperative, risk-seeking or risk avers, error-embracing or error avoiding, productive or defensive." This theoretically maps to leadership communication concepts and power structures within the organization.

Lewin's introduction of unfreezing and freezing behaviors dynamically relates to the learning and unlearning of behaviors in the organization. Argyris believes that individuals within the organization have systems of learning developed internally. This is the definition of Argyris's concepts of Theories-in-use. These theories are the systems shaped by the environment individuals grow up in and live in. That theory dictates the desire to learn on an individual level basis is the individual's theory-in-use. This concept is highlighted by Argyris from Bateson (1972) work determining that organizations have deuterolearning. The definition developed by Bateson aligns to double-loop learning, where the individuals learn to learn. Argyris refers to this as the process of the individual moving from Model I to Model II.

Argyris elaborates on Model I structure by highlighting the work of Dewey, in reference to the concepts of inquiry. Dewey defines inquiry as psychological analysis and movement, where individuals result in some type of transactional process by being a participant in seeking clarity and modifying the information. The action should output some learning. The process is an open system that loops back. The constraint is the defensive process that prohibits the looping and inquiry of information presented. I bring this information forward to establish the concept that organizational implementation failures take place based on the individual's Theory-in-use. I want to connect the Theories-in-use process to dysfunctional organizations and the implementations of organizational development.

3) Application and Strategies

In the process of developing strategic application, I will use Gibson's *et al* model as a baseline. In understanding external drivers, I will use SWOT and the three areas that Gibson *et al.* uses structure, technology, and process. SWOT is the market analysis for understanding where your corporation is in relation to your competitor. For example in identifying your companies "structural"; strengths, weakness, opportunities and threats: "technical"; strengths, weakness, opportunities, and threats:, as well as "process"; strengths, weakness, opportunities, and threats. Gibson *et al* then moves to reviewing performance outcomes on an organizational, group, and individual level. The purpose of integrating the SWOT concept with the evaluation of internal goal performance gives a detail view of either structural SWOT issues and/or process

SWOT issues. Either outcome can lead to a thorough review of a technical SWOT analysis. One would unlikely have data referring to any activities of their competitor's internal organization, therefore general goals achievement analysis works for performance review. Competitor information shared is that of products, profit, and losses. Yet, summations of that information and market best practices can be used to stream line the evaluation.

Where SWOT reflects external forces imposed on the company, the internal forces exist as initiatives. The creation of initiatives focuses efforts in the improvement of internal process. The implementation of such changes requires a variety of system analysis. System analysis includes understanding employee structure and employee needs. The emphases on productivity and effectivity improvements lie in internal initiatives.

The impact of present performance review allows leadership to see and acknowledge the complexity of the organization. The expected outcome relates to evaluating organizational changes that may be required. The process provides data to work flow issues, job design issues, hierarchical issues, or overall structural issues. The need to review rework processes and failures in the system allows for correction to those systems. The impact of such failures ultimately contributes or subtracts from profits.

In step three, Gibson *et al.* completes a diagnosis of the problems, where I would suggest in addition to completing a diagnostic review management should perform a gap analysis. In the model, I am presenting a general diagnosis process building on the data from the SWOT or Porter's Force Five. Based on that concept this is market review and presently there are no indicators of actual failure, the need to understand the surrounding environment is important. This is a method to anticipate change needs. In this step, issues will arise. The requirement is to develop strategic methods to limit or eliminate the organizational issues. I would suggest that by implementing Gibson's *et al.* you might introduce more organizational stresses and anxiety thereby creating a dysfunctional organization. I propose that structuring the process of diagnosis in a format that focuses on an area such as organization make contradictions more identifiable. By analyzing the organization for function and dysfunction, outliers will present themselves. In any organization, structure creation and enhancements have purpose. Truly, the initial implementation of any organizational restructure focuses its energy in alignment for productivity and effectivity.

There is a realistic relationship between the organization and leadership. Problems developed within the leadership structure affect the organization. Detection of issues early allows the development of counter measures with the appropriate means for action. A data collection method is surveying.

There are many methods developed today to assist in the analysis of the organization. My suggestion would be to use the tools described in this section for organizational or individual diagnosis. On an individual level, Baurch and Lambert's (2007) article describes a model using psychological systems implementation. Baurch *et al.* includes an appraisal process, which allows the change agent to understand the environment and the organization. This is to determine the impact on the individual. Baurch *et al.* reviews three focus areas in his model. These areas are and align to functions in psychological analysis of individuals:

- "Internal process response"="Biological Responses"
- "Organizational Trust"="Psychological Responses"
- "Organizational Practice"="Behavioral Responses"

This model develops coping mechanisms to anxiety within an organization. The process is to guide in the cultivating life skills for handling difficult situations. The model allows the change agent to review stimulus process to individual within the organization. The model applications can be individual or organizational. The next model I would suggest is more specific to analyzing organizations. This system's development authors are Balthazard, Cooke, and Potter (2006). Balthazard's *et al.* system reviews behavioral norms within the organization, which contribute to the organizational culture. The model builds an inventory of these norms within a study called Organizational Culture Inventory (OCI). This system focuses on three observable core styles in organizational systems. These are constructive, passive/defensive, and aggressive/defensive. This system usage is globally recommended to understand an organizations structured culture. The system measures 12 behavioral norms concerning the core styles. Balthazard *et al.* defines each core style in as:

- "Constructive norms promote achievement-oriented and cooperative behaviors which should promote a individual outcomes

such as satisfaction, organizational outcomes including quality of service, and ultimately knowledge management processes."
- "Defensive norms create pressures for dependent and avoidant (passive) and/or power-oriented and internally competitive styles (aggressive) and, in turn, are dysfunctional for both the organization and its members."

A style analysis will highlight patterns within organizations. The output of the data allows the change agent to develop an implementable solution to create a more constructive environment. An additional model, from Fleet and Griffin (2006), focuses on the impact of leadership in creating a dysfunctional organization. The results are negative employee behaviors. This model analyzes the individual predisposition to take part in negative behavior, which inturn evolves into a dysfunctional organization. The framework developed centers around a cube like tool that measures the individual tendencies to contribute to an organization negatively and the organization's action to those tendencies. If the individual and organization reside in quadrant 2 there may be a need for action on the part of the organization. Below is the framework developed from Fleet (2006, pp703).

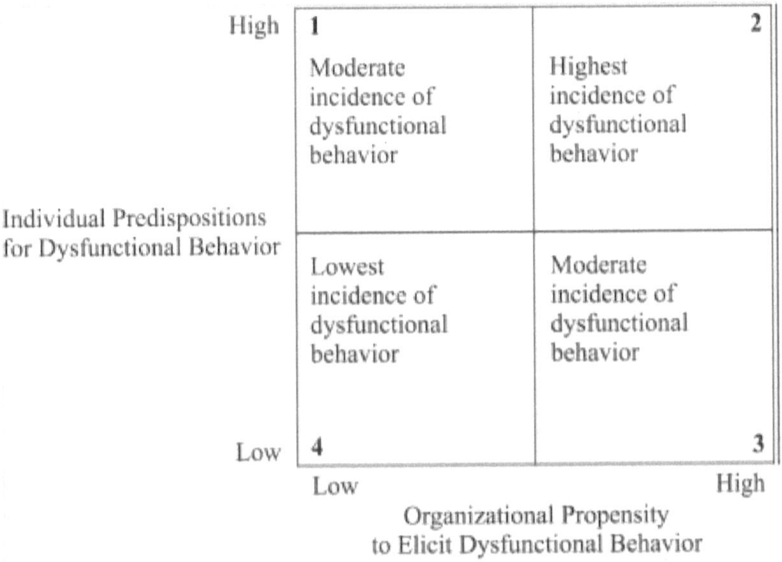

Individual Predispositions for Dysfunctional Behavior		
High	1. Moderate incidence of dysfunctional behavior	2. Highest incidence of dysfunctional behavior
Low	4. Lowest incidence of dysfunctional behavior	3. Moderate incidence of dysfunctional behavior
	Low	High

Organizational Propensity to Elicit Dysfunctional Behavior

Source: Adapted from Griffin and Lopez (2004)

Figure 1 Fleet and Griffin's Model

Each model provides the change agent with diagnostic tools at various levels. In any event understanding the implementation environment is helpful data and moves the process closer to success.

The next step for Gibson *et al* is the selection of an implementation, I consider at this point to understand constraint to the implementation process. Constraints could include management or leadership value systems. The presence of constraints in leadership could indicate dysfunction within the organization. The need is to attempt to have a successful implementation of the change with little to no looping back for correction. In a dysfunctional organization, some of this data is unrevealed until the implementation, which is the purpose for looping back. Generally, the lack of information makes it difficult to unfreeze behaviors.

To build a complete model I wanted to included, alignment with the company's overall business, organization, and individual goals. Understanding the finish point of the organization aids in the development of the system execution. Very few change management systems account for potential goal achievement, they focus rather on how well the organization performed on past goals.

The final steps are implementation and feedback. The models I have highlighted are new to organizational change and provide the industry with broaden landscapes of understanding. In the knowledge age industry, people require more to feel satisfied. This application aids the organization in learning about itself as an organization and creating knowledge for better system implementations. The knowledge gathered from individuals is useful in evolving the organization into learning individuals. These concepts are applicable with the standard needs of an organization. Those needs align to individual needs for recognition and inclusiveness.

By completing step three of this process, many answers to questions with the organization become clear. I would then suggest developing tactical program and plans to meet the gaps. The needs for inclusiveness and openness have solutions in the creating implementations. In developing tactical plans, the SWOT method is useful. It gives the change agent a high-level view of areas in need. Below is an illustration of the model I am proposing.

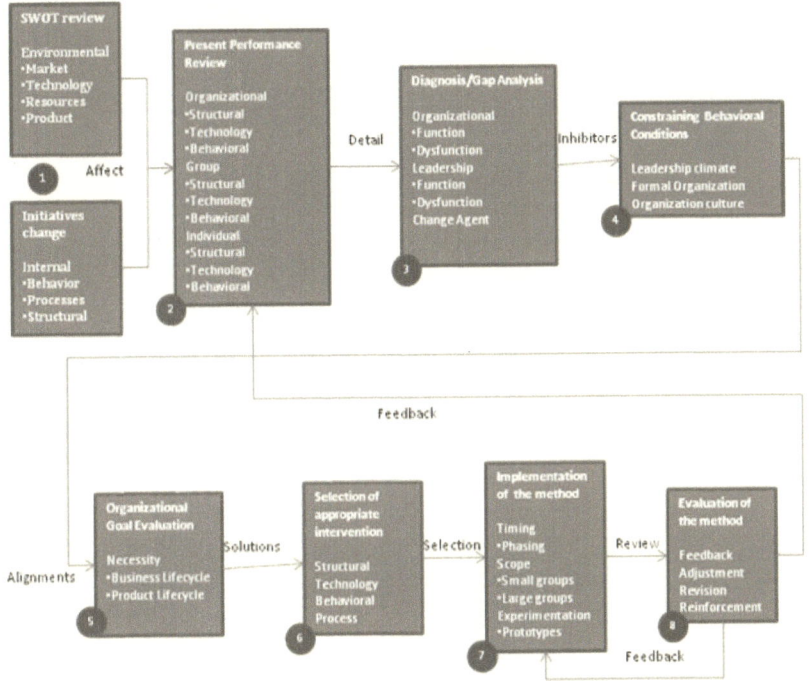

Figure 2 Organizational Change Model

III. Summary

This model attempts to include the individual psychological impacts to organizational change. The model brings to light issues that occur on either level. The reason for organizational change and development is improvement. Improvements of the performance of individuals to that of the organization, the impact of such improvement appear in the profits of the company. The desire to have larger profits drives us to desiring learning organizations and the implementation of such environments can destroy a company. Many companies are keenly aware of their positions in organizational lifecycles and business lifecycles. The need for change shall be a constant in the life of the company.

REFERENCE

Abrams, L., Conway, M., Lipsky, D., Slepian, J., Wirtenberg, J., (2007). The Future of Organization Development: Enabling Sustainable Business Performance Through People. Organization Development Journal, 25, 2, 11-22.

Argyris, C. (1990). Overcoming Organizational Defenses: Needham Heights, MA.: Allyn-Bacon.

Anderson, M. & Associates (2000). Fast Cycle Organizational Development: Cincinnati, OH.: South-Western College Publishing.

Bacigaluop, A., Blattner, J., (2007). Using Emotional Intelligence to Develop Executive Leadership and Team and Organizational Development. Consulting Psychology Journal: Practice and Research, 59, 3, 209-219.

Balthazard, P. A., Cooke, R. A., Potter, R. E., (2006). Dysfunctional culture, dysfunctional organization: Capturing the behavioral norms that form organizational culture and drive performance. Journal of Managerial Psychology, 21, 8, 709-732.

Baurch, Y., Lambert, J., (2007). Organizational anxiety: applying psychological concepts into organizational theory. Journal of Managerial Psychology, 22, 1, 84-99.

Blau, G., Andersson, L., Davis, K., Daymont, T., Hochner, A. Koziara, K., Portwood, J. Holladay, B., (2008). The relation between employee organizational and professional development activities. Journal of Vocational Behavior, 72, 1, 123-142.

Burke, W.W. (1994). Organizational Development: A Process of Learning and Changing: Reading, Mass.: Addison-Wesley Publishing.

Coughlan, P., Suri, J. F., Canales, K. Prototypes as (Design) Tools for Behavioral and Organizational Change. The Journal of Applied Behavior Science, 43, 1, 122-134.

Covey, S., (2007). Organizational Development. Journal of Training, 44, 4, 40-40.

Donnenberg, O., De Loo, I., (2004). Facilitating Organizational development through action learning-some practical and theoretical considerations. Action Learning: Research and Practice, 1, 2, 167-184.

Etzioni, A. (1964). Modern organizations. Engelwood Cliff, NJ: Prentice Hall.

Etzioni, A. (1975). A comparative analysis of complex organizations: On power, involvement, and their correlates. (Rev. and enl. ed.). New York: Free Press.

Gibson, J. L., Ivancevich, J. M. & Donnelly, J. H. (1976). Organizations: Behavior, structure and process. (Rev. ed.) Dallas, TX: Business Publications.

Goldman, A., (2006). High toxicity leadership: Borderline personality disorder and the dysfunctional organization. Journal of Managerial Psychology, 21, 8, 733-746.

Goldman, A., (2006). Personality disorders in leaders: Implications of the DSM IV-TR in assessing dysfunctional organizations. Journal of Managerial Psychology, 21, 5, 392-414.

Hall, R. H. (2002). Organizations: Structures, processes, and outcomes. (8th ed.). Upper Saddle River, NJ: Prentice Hall.

Knowles, M. & Knowles, H. (1966). Introduction to Group Dynamics: New York, N.Y.: Associate Press.

Kohler, J. M., Munz, D.C., (2006). Combining Individual and Organizational Stress Intervention, An Organizational Development Approach. Consulting Psychology Journal: Practice and Research, 58, 1, 1-12.

Kruppa, R., Meda, A. K. (2005). Group Dynamics in the Formation of 0PhD Cohort: A Reflection in Experiencing. Organization Development Journal, 23, 1, 56-67.

Langer, A. M., (2005). Responsive Organizational dynamism: managing technolory using reflective practice. Reflective Practice, 6,2, 247-254.

Lowry, C., (2005). Continuous Organizational Development – Teamwork, Learning Leadership and Measurement. Libraries and the Academy, 5, 1, 1-6.

McLean, G., (2005). Doing Organization Development in Complex Systems: The case at a Large U.S. Research, Land Grant University. Advances in Developing Human Resources, 7, 3, 311-323.

Morgan, G. (1997). Images of organizations. (Rev. ed.). Thousand Oaks, CA:Sage.

Phipps, S. E.,(2004). The System Design Approach to Organizational Development: The University of Arizona Model. Library Trends, 53, 1, 68-111.

van Fleet, D. D., Griffin, R. W., (2006). Dysfunctional organization culture: The role of leadership in motivating dysfunctional work behaviors. Journal of Managerial Psychology, 21, 8, 698-708.

www.ingramcontent.com/pod-product-compliance
Lightning Source LLC
Chambersburg PA
CBHW021009180526
45163CB00005B/1945